THE DEMANDS OF REASON

The Demands of Reason

An Essay on Pyrrhonian Scepticism

CASEY PERIN

OXFORD

UNIVERSITY PRESS

OXFORD
UNIVERSITY PRESS

Great Clarendon Street, Oxford, OX2 6DP,
United Kingdom

Oxford University Press is a department of the University of Oxford.
It furthers the University's objective of excellence in research, scholarship,
and education by publishing worldwide. Oxford is a registered trade mark of
Oxford University Press in the UK and in certain other countries

Published in the United States of America by Oxford University Press
198 Madison Avenue, New York, NY 10016, United States of America

British Library Cataloguing in Publication Data
Data available

Library of Congress Control Number: 2010920517

ISBN 978-0-19-955790-5

For Sarah and Max

Acknowledgements

I want to thank Richard Bett and a second, anonymous, reader for Oxford University Press for their extensive and constructive comments on this book. I'm grateful to Katja Vogt and Nishi Shah for both their comments on the manuscript as well as their encouragement. I owe a special debt to Peter Momtchiloff of Oxford University Press for his interest in the project from its earliest stages, his patience, and his flexibility. I very much appreciate the efforts of Tessa Eaton, my production editor at Oxford, Catherine Berry, Abigail Coulson, and my copy-editor Edwin Pritchard.

An earlier, and shorter, version of Chapter 1 appeared as 'Pyrrhonian Scepticism and the Search for Truth' in *Oxford Studies in Ancient Philosophy* 30 (Summer 2006), 337–60.

Contents

Introduction

Pyrrhonian scepticism had a long history in antiquity, and in the course of that history it assumed several very different forms.[1] In this book I shall be concerned exclusively with Pyrrhonian scepticism as it is presented by Sextus Empiricus in his *Outlines of Pyrrhonism*.[2] The *Outlines* is complete in three books. In its second and third books Sextus surveys, and argues against, a variety of views in each of the three parts into which post-Aristotelian philosophy was standardly divided by its practioners: logic (encompassing much of what we today think of as epistemology), physics (including metaphysics), and ethics. In the first book of the *Outlines*, by contrast, Sextus offers a completely general account of Scepticism.[3] In doing so he provides a definition of Scepticism (*PH* 1.8); he identifies its aim (*PH* 1.25–6) and the principles that motivate it (*PH* 1.12); he makes some remarkably cryptic remarks about its scope (*PH* 1.13, 1.19–20); he introduces the criterion or standard (κριτήριον) by which the Sceptic's actions are guided (*PH* 1.21–4); he

---

[1] On Pyrrho (*c*.360–*c*.270 BCE), the eponymous figurehead of Pyrrhonian scepticism, see especially Sedley, 'The Motivation of Greek Skepticism', 14–15 and 20–1; and, for a comprehensive discussion of Pyrrho and his connections to later versions of Pyrrhonian scepticism, see Bett, *Pyrrho, his Antecedents, and his Legacy*. On Aenesidemus, a Pyrrhonian sceptic from the first century BCE, see Woodruff, 'Aporetic Pyrrhonism'.

[2] This work is standardly referred to by the abbreviation *PH* derived from its Greek title. References to it are by book and section number. We know next to nothing about Sextus himself. A series of plausible conjectures support the conclusion that he was active in the second century AD. In addition to the *Outlines* we possess two other works by Sextus. Due to an error in the manuscript tradition, however, both of these works have come down to us under the title *Against the Learned* (often referred to by its Latin title *Adversus Mathematicos* or by the abbreviation *M*). References to this work are, again, by book and section number. *Against the Learned* Books 7–11—a work Sextus himself seems to have called *Sceptical Treatises* (τὰ σκεπτικὰ ὑπομνήματα, see *M* 1.29, 2.106, 6.52)— covers the same broad range of philosophical topics, though often at greater length, as *Outlines* Books 2–3. The work known as *Against the Learned* Books 1–6 is a critical examination of grammar, rhetoric, geometry, arithmetic, astronomy, and music.

[3] I use 'Scepticism' with a capital 'S' to designate the form of Pyrrhonian scepticism described by Sextus in the *Outlines*.

rehearses at some length the different modes (τρόποι) or argument forms by which the Sceptic comes to suspend judgement about any matter he investigates (*PH* 1.31–186); he explains how certain utterances the Sceptic routinely makes are to be understood (*PH* 1.187–208); and he distinguishes Scepticism from those philosophical views or sects with which it might be confused (*PH* 1.210–41).

My treatment of this material is highly selective. There are a number of important features of Scepticism as Sextus describes it in the *Outlines* to which I pay little or no attention. For example, I do not consider in any detail the ten modes of suspension of judgement that, according to Sextus, are the work of Aenesidemus.[4] Nor do I offer any extended discussion of the so-called Agrippan modes—the small set of argument forms particular instances of which occur throughout Sextus' writings.[5] Moreover, I say nothing about Sextus' arguments against causal explanation or about the merits of his arguments against those dogmatic philosophical views he examines.[6] And, finally, I make no attempt to map out the complex relations between Scepticism and the Empirical school of medicine.[7] In the following four chapters I examine those aspects of Scepticism—its commitment to the search for truth and to certain principles of rationality, its scope, and its consequences for action and agency—that seem to me at least to be of special philosophical significance.

There is no philosophical view someone must have in order to be a Sceptic, and in fact Sextus says that the Sceptic does not have any philosophical views at all. Nonetheless, according to Sextus, Scepticism, along with positive and negative dogmatism, is one of the three most fundamental kinds of philosophy (αἱ ἀνωτάτω φιλοσοφίαι *PH* 1.4). The positive dogmatist is someone who claims to have discovered the truth in some area of philosophical inquiry and, as a result, has positive philosophical views. The negative dogmatist, too, has a philosophical

---

[4] Sextus at *M* 7.345 attributes the ten modes to Aenesidemus. For a general discussion of these modes, see Striker, 'The Ten Tropes of Aenesidemus', and Annas and Barnes, *The Modes of Scepticism*.

[5] At *PH* 1.164 Sextus attributes these modes to what he calls 'the more recent Sceptics' (οἱ νεώτεροι σκεπτικοί) that are identified by Diogenes Laertius (9.88–9) as Agrippa and his school (οἱ περὶ Ἀγρίππαν). For an exemplary discussion of the Agrippan modes, see Barnes, *The Toils of Scepticism*.

[6] On Sextus' arguments against causal explanation, see Barnes, 'Ancient Skepticism and Causation'.

[7] On these topics see Frede, 'The Ancient Empiricists', and Allen, *Inferences from Signs*, 87–146.

view, but it is the view that the truth cannot be discovered and that knowledge of one or more kinds is impossible.[8] The Sceptic is different from both the positive and the negative dogmatist insofar as he neither claims to have discovered the truth nor denies that it is possible to do so. But if, as Sextus claims, Scepticism is a kind of philosophy, then it must also have something in common with both positive and negative dogmatism in virtue of which it is, like them, a kind of philosophy. Yet the only thing Scepticism has in common with positive and negative dogmatism is that the Sceptic is engaged in the activity of searching for the truth—a Sceptic (σκεπτικός) is, quite literally, one who invesitages or inquires (σκέπτεται)—and this is an activity in which both the positive and the negative dogmatist were once but are no longer engaged. If this is right, then for Sextus philosophy just is the search for truth or, perhaps more precisely, the search for the truth about certain matters. Someone is a philosopher, in turn, if she *is* engaged in the search for truth or, alternatively, *was* so engaged but, at least as it seemed to her, made a discovery that brought the search to an end. And that was either the discovery of the truth for which she was searching or the discovery that this truth cannot be discovered.

Sextus' claim that Scepticism is a kind of philosophy, and that this is so because the Sceptic is engaged in the search for truth, has struck many as dubious. And this, principally, for two reasons. First, according to Sextus the Sceptic is able to achieve his ultimate end, tranquillity (ἀταραξία), through suspension of judgement (ἐποχή). Yet if the Sceptic has this ability, and *if* he values the discovery of truth only as a means to achieving tranquillity, then the Sceptic has no reason at all to engage in the search for truth. For the discovery of truth is neither the necessary nor the most efficient means to the Sceptic's ultimate end. Second, the Sceptic routinely uses arguments—the Agrippan modes—that purport to show that no one can have any reason to believe anything. The use of arguments with this negative dogmatic conclusion seems to be incompatible with genuine engagement in the search for truth. For a person is

---

[8] At *PH* 1.4 Sextus says that the three most fundamental kinds of philosophy are 'Dogmatic, Academic, and Sceptical' (δογματικὴ Ἀκαδημαϊκὴ σκεπτική). But Sextus' identification of negative dogmatism with Academic philosophy is unhelpful in at least two respects. First, it is far from clear in our sources, and so a matter of interpretation, whether the Academics, and especially Arcesilaus and Carneades, were negative dogmatists. (Sextus himself seems reluctant to count Arcesilaus as a negative dogmatist. See *PH* 1.232.) Second, Sextus himself counts philosophers who are not Academics—e.g. the Cyrenaics—as negative dogmatists. See *PH* 1.215.

genuinely engaged in the search for the truth about some matter only if she does not deny that it is possible to discover the truth about that matter. But, it is claimed, insofar as the Sceptic uses the Agrippan modes he is committed to the view that the truth about the matters he investigates cannot be discovered and, consequently, that the search for truth is futile. In Chapter 1 I argue that Sextus can answer these criticisms. I do so by explaining *why*, according to Sextus, the Sceptic engages in the search for truth and *how* it is possible for the Sceptic to do so while using, as he does, the Agrippan modes.

The Sceptic's search for truth is supposed to lead to, but not terminate in, suspension of judgement. The Sceptic suspends judgement about whether *p* if and only if it appears to him that he has no reason to believe either *p* or its negation. It is a striking fact that Sextus often describes the Sceptic's suspension of judgement as a matter of *necessity*. For Sextus often writes not that the Sceptic *does* or *will* suspend judgement about whether *p*, but that it is *necessary*, or that he is *compelled*, to do so. In Chapter 2 I examine the kind of necessity Sextus has in view when he describes the Sceptic's suspension of judgement in this way. I argue that the Sceptic aims to satisfy a certain rational requirement and that the fact that he does so is the source of the necessity that is attached to his suspension of judgement. This necessity is in the first instance hypothetical: it is necessary for the Sceptic to suspend judgement *if* he is to satisfy, as he aims to do, the demands of reason. I then argue that the Sceptic has the aim of satisfying certain rational requirements because part of what it is to be engaged in the search for truth, as Sextus claims the Sceptic is, is to have this aim.

The scope of Scepticism is the range of candidates for belief about which the Sceptic, in virtue of being a Sceptic, suspends judgement. Sextus places a restriction on the Sceptic's suspension of judgement, and so on the scope of Scepticism, insofar as he attributes, as I argue he does at *PH* 1.13, some beliefs (δόγματα) to the Sceptic. As a result an adequate interpretation of the scope of Scepticism must draw a distinction between two kinds of belief. Call a belief of the kind the Sceptic, in virtue of his Scepticism, lacks a *dogmatic belief*; and call a belief of the kind his Scepticism permits him to have a *non-dogmatic belief*. In Chapter 3 I argue, against a prominent recent line of interpretation, that for Sextus the distinction between dogmatic and non-dogmatic belief is the distinction between belief about how things *are* and belief about how things merely *appear* to one to be. A close reading of *PH* 1.13 reveals that, according to Sextus, the Sceptic suspends judgement

universally about how things are and has beliefs only abou ↻
appear to him to be.

If this is the scope of Scepticism—if, that is, the Sceptic ha
about how things are rather than merely appear to him to
Scepticism invites the objection that the Sceptic cannot act. I
requires beliefs of the very kind the Sceptic, in virtue of being a ⌐ptic,
lacks, namely, beliefs about how things are. Yet if the Sceptic cannot act,
then Scepticism is not, as Sextus claims it is, a possible way of life. And if
the Sceptic does act, then the fact that he does so indicates that he has
beliefs about how things are and so is not, after all, a Sceptic. This is the
well-known *apraxia* or inaction argument against Scepticism, and its
conclusion is that Scepticism is incompatible with action. In Chapter 4
I distinguish two versions of the *apraxia* argument. Sextus explicitly
replies to the version of the argument according to which Scepticism is
incompatible with activity or behaviour of any kind. I outline Sextus'
reply to this version of the *apraxia* argument and claim that it is
adequate only if Sextus can provide some account of the difference
between an appearance—the kind of psychological state that, according
to Sextus, guides the Sceptic's actions—and a belief. I attempt to make
clear that providing an account of this sort is no small task.

A second version of the *apraxia* argument challenges not the existence
but the status of the Sceptic's activities and takes as its starting point a
theory of action that draws a distinction between *action* and *mere activity*
or *bodily movement*. Sextus does not reply to this version of the *apraxia*
argument, but it is the version the Stoics advanced against the Academics and their recommendation that a person suspend judgement about
everything. The Stoics, unsurprisingly, took their own theory of action
as a starting point. In Chapter 4 I consider whether Sextus has the
resources to reply to this second version of the *apraxia* argument when it
starts not from the Stoic theory of action but from the now more or less
standard belief-desire model of action. According to this model an
action is the doing of something for a reason, and doing something
for a reason is a matter of one's activity or behaviour being motivated,
and therefore caused, in the right way (whatever that is) by a combination of a belief and a desire. I explore whether and how the Sceptic can
grant that action is the doing of something for a reason but argue that
doing something for a reason, and so acting rather than merely being
active, does *not* require beliefs of the kind the Sceptic lacks.

I have come to think that a comprehensive interpretation of Scepticism—an interpretation that makes the way of life and the kind of

philosophy described in the *Outlines of Pyrrhonism* fully coherent—is not possible. Sextus stands at the end of a long and complex philosophical tradition, and he includes in the *Outlines* material from distinct, and sometimes conflicting, phases of that tradition. Nonetheless, it seems to me that in the *Outlines* some features or aspects of Scepticism are far more prominent than others. Scepticism is sometimes characterized by commentators as a form of anti-rationalism. It is claimed that the Sceptic renounces reason as a guide to thought and action. The Sceptic's motive for doing so is said to be either the negative dogmatism to which his arguments commit him (Sextus' claims to the contrary notwithstanding) or a view he holds about the conditions under which tranquillity, the Sceptic's ultimate objective, can be achieved. In the Conclusion I try to explain briefly, and by appealing to arguments I make in the course of the book, why it seems to me that this line of interpretation fails to capture what is most central to Scepticism.[9]

[9] Throughout I use, often modified, the translation in Annas and Barnes, *Outlines*.

I want to argue that's by design.

1

The Search for Truth

Scepticism as Sextus presents it is not a philosophical view but, strange as it may seem, a way of life (ἀγωγή *PH* 1.16–17). Two passages at the outset of the *Outlines of Pyrrhonism* raise fundamental issues about Scepticism as a way of life:

When people are investigating any subject, the likely result is either a discovery, or a denial of discovery and a confession of unknowability (ἀκαταληψίας ὁμολογίαν), or else a continuation of the investigation (ἐπιμονὴν ζητήσεως). This, no doubt, is why in the case of philosophical investigations, too, some have said that they have discovered the truth, some have asserted that it cannot be known, and others are still investigating (οἱ δὲ ἔτι ζητοῦσιν). Those who are called Dogmatists in the proper sense of the word think they have discovered the truth—for example, the schools of Aristotle and Epicurus and the Stoics, and some others. The schools of Clitomachus and Carneades, and other Academics, have asserted that things cannot be known. And the Sceptics are investigating (ζητοῦσι δὲ οἱ Σκεπτικοί). (*PH* 1.1–3)

The Sceptical way of life (ἡ σκεπτικὴ ἀγωγή), then, is also called 'Investigative' (ζητητική), from its activity in investigating and inquiring (ἀπὸ ἐνεργείας τῆς κατὰ τὸ ζητεῖν καὶ σκέπτεσθαι); 'Suspensive' (ἐφεκτική), from the condition that comes about in the inquirer after the investigation (μετὰ τὴν ζήτησιν); 'Perplexed' (ἀπορητική), either (as some say) from the fact that it is perplexed about and investigates everything (ἀπὸ τοῦ περὶ παντὸς ἀπορεῖν καὶ ζητεῖν), or else from its being at a loss (ἀπὸ τοῦ ἀμηχανεῖν) whether to assent or deny. (*PH* 1.7)

usually
'aporetic'

The Sceptical way of life is at least in part a life of philosophical investigation, and Sextus says that it differs in this respect from the way of life exemplified by the dogmatic philosopher. For investigation has no place in the life of the dogmatic philosopher—either because he claims to have discovered the truth about the matters that are of interest to him and so has no need to investigate them, or because he denies that it is possible to discover the truth about such matters and so in his view no investigation can succeed. The Sceptic, by contrast, neither claims to have discovered the truth about the matters he investigates nor denies that it is possible to do so. That fact, according to Sextus, explains why investigation is an option for the Sceptic but not for the dogmatic philosopher. But, as Sextus indicates elsewhere (*PH* 1.12, 1.25–9), it is the Sceptic's desire for tranquillity, together with the fact that it appears to him that he can achieve tranquillity by discovering the truth, that explains why the Sceptic exercises this option.

The Sceptic, then, is someone who investigates, and to investigate a matter is, according to Sextus, to search for the truth about it. In fact I doubt whether investigation can be understood as anything but the search for truth, but I am claiming here only that investigation as Sextus understands it—the activity he claims the Sceptic is engaged in—is the search for truth. Now it is true that neither in *PH* 1.1–3 nor in *PH* 1.7 does Sextus *explicitly* characterize the Sceptic's investigation as the search for truth. But it seems to me the clear implication of *PH* 1.1–3 (as of *PH* 2.1, a passage I discuss later in this chapter) is that the Sceptic's investigation is to be characterized in this way. First, Sextus in *PH* 1.1–3 (as in *PH* 2.1) employs a *single* conception of investigation, and he must do so if his claim that the Sceptic, unlike the dogmatic philosopher, is *still* investigating is to make any sense at all. That claim is the claim that the Sceptic is still doing *the very thing* the dogmatic philosopher is no longer doing. Second, Sextus says that both the discovery of truth and the discovery that the truth cannot be discovered (which, of course, is itself the discovery of a truth) are possible outcomes of the investigation in which the Sceptic is still, but the dogmatic philosopher no longer, engaged. In fact Sextus implies that the dogmatic philosopher is no longer engaged in investigation precisely *because* he has either discovered the truth or has discovered that the truth cannot be discovered. But *these* discoveries can terminate an investigation only if that investigation is the search for truth. So if the Sceptic is still engaged in the sort of investigation that the dogmatic philosopher has either concluded or abandoned, as Sextus claims he is, then the Sceptic is, as the dogmatic philosopher once was, engaged in the search for truth. And the Sceptic is so engaged because it appears to him that the discovery of truth is a means to the tranquillity that is, according to Sextus, his ultimate objective.

Some of his modern readers, as well as certain critics in antiquity, have argued that Sextus' description of the Sceptic as engaged in the search for truth is a sham.[1] Sextus himself defines Scepticism as the

---

[1] For Sextus' unnamed critics in antiquity, see *PH* 2.1; and for their modern counterparts, see especially J. Palmer, 'Skeptical Investigation', Striker, 'Scepticism as a Kind

ability to achieve tranquillity through suspension of judgement (
1.8). If the Sceptic is by definition someone who has this ability, t‖
the Sceptic need not discover the truth in order to achieve tranquillity—
the discovery of truth is not, for the Sceptic at least, a necessary means to
tranquillity. Yet if the Sceptic can achieve tranquillity *either* by discovering the truth *or* by suspending judgement, and *if* the Sceptic values the
discovery of truth only as a means to tranquillity, then the Sceptic has no
reason to pursue tranquillity by means of the discovery of truth rather
than by means of suspension of judgement. In fact, if the ability to
achieve tranquillity through suspension of judgement is constitutive of
Scepticism, as Sextus claims it is, then part of what it is to be a Sceptic
rather than a non-Sceptic is to pursue tranquillity by means of suspension of judgement rather than by some other means like the discovery
of truth. If this is right, then the Sceptic is and must be someone who is
not engaged in the search for truth. In addition, the Sceptic deploys
instances of certain argument-schemas—the so-called Agrippan
modes—that collectively purport to show that no one can have any
reason to believe anything. But the use of arguments with this negative
dogmatic conclusion seems to be incompatible with the search for truth.
For someone is *genuinely* engaged in the search for the truth about some
matter only if she does not deny that it is possible to discover the truth
about that matter. Someone who denies that it is possible to discover the
truth for which she is searching is not really searching for that truth but
at most acting as if she is. And to search for the truth is to search for
reasons for belief, that is, considerations that count as reasons for
believing one thing rather than another about the matter under investigation. Someone who denies that one can have any reason to believe
anything, as the Sceptic appears to do by using the Agrippan modes,
thereby denies that it is possible to discover *any* truth. Yet if the Sceptic
denies *this*, then he is, regardless of Sextus' claims to the contrary, a
negative dogmatist, and the completely general scope of his negative
dogmatism prevents him from being engaged in the search for *any* truth.

These criticisms are important but, I shall argue, misplaced. In this ⟨good⟩
chapter I first survey a number of texts in which, according to some
commentators, Sextus' description of the Sceptic or his arguments

of Philosophy', and (largely following Palmer and Striker on this issue) Grgic, 'Sextus
Empiricus and the Goal of Skepticism'. See Brennan, *Ethics and Epistemology in Sextus
Empiricus*, 84–7 and 99–106, for a defence of the claim that the Sceptic is engaged in the
search for truth.

conflicts with the claim that the Sceptic is engaged in the search for truth. My task here is largely negative: I attempt to show that these texts need not and should not be read in this way. But the completion of that negative task leaves unanswered the two important questions raised by these criticisms. So I next try to explain *why*, according to Sextus, the Sceptic—that is, someone who can achieve tranquillity through suspension of judgement—engages in the search for truth and *how* the Sceptic's use of the Agrippan modes is compatible with his doing so.

On one line of interpretation the Sceptic abandons the search for truth on the grounds that it cannot succeed. Thus Louis Loeb has written that although the Sceptic initially aims to achieve tranquillity by discovering the truth, 'the lower-order aim of truth is renounced as one that cannot be achieved and the higher-order objective of quietude is achieved in another way, by suspending belief'.[2] But Loeb's view here cannot be right, and this for at least two reasons. First, the Sceptic has no grounds for claiming that the search for truth *cannot* succeed. (Nor does Sextus anywhere in the *Outlines* report that the Sceptic takes himself to have grounds for making this claim.) It is true that up to now his investigations have concluded in suspension of judgement, but *that* fact, as the Sceptic himself recognizes, is no reason to deny that it is *possible* to discover the truth. Second, if, as Loeb claims, the Sceptic abandons the search for truth on the grounds that it cannot succeed, then Scepticism collapses into a form of negative dogmatism. Yet Sextus takes great care to distinguish the Sceptic from those negative dogmatists (according to Sextus, the Academics, the Cyrenaics, and the Empiricist school of medicine) who deny that the truth about the matters investigated by philosophers can be known (*PH* 1.3, 1.200, 1.215, 1.226, 1.236). The Sceptic suspends judgement about whether it is possible to discover the truth, and the fact that the Sceptic does so is enough to distinguish him from those who deny that it is possible to discover the truth.

Sextus does tell us, however, that *some* Sceptics make suspension of judgement one of their objectives. At the conclusion of his discussion of the Sceptic's end or goal (τέλος), Sextus writes that

we say that the Sceptic's end or goal (τέλος τοῦ Σκεπτικοῦ) is tranquillity in matters of belief and moderation in the conditions forced on him. Some prominent Sceptics have added to these [ends or goals] suspension of judgement in

    ² Loeb, 'Sextus, Descartes, Hume, and Peirce: On Securing Settled Doxastic States', 214.

doxastic
continuum.

investigations (προσέθηκαν τούτοις καὶ τὴν ἐν ταῖς ζητήσεσιν ⟨ (*PH* 1.30)[3]

According to Diogenes Laertius (9.107) these prominent Scep clude Timon and Aenesidemus, and Sextus suggests here that they pursue suspension of judgement as a means to achieving tranquillity. For these Sceptics are said to have identified suspension of judgement as an end or goal *in addition to* tranquillity, and there is no indication in Sextus' text, and no reason to think, that suspension of judgement has some value for these Sceptics independently of its relation to tranquillity. Moreover, Sextus alludes to these Sceptics again in his discussion of the sceptical phrase 'opposed to every account there is an equal account' (περὶ τοῦ παντὶ λόγῳ λόγον ἴσον ἀντικεῖσθαι). Sextus explains that those who follow the version of Scepticism he is presenting in the *Outlines* utter this phrase to report that they are in the condition (πάθος) in which it appears to them that every dogmatic account they have examined up to now in support of a given candidate for belief is opposed by some equally credible dogmatic account in support of a conflicting candidate for belief (*PH* 1.203). But, Sextus adds, some Sceptics utter this phrase as an exhortation to other sceptics to oppose to every dogmatic account they encounter a second, conflicting dogmatic account equal in credibility to the first. Sextus writes that

They make this exhortation to the Sceptic to prevent him from being seduced by the dogmatists into abandoning his investigation and through rashness missing the tranquillity apparent to him, which (as we suggested before) they think follows on suspension of judgement about everything (ἣν νομίζουσι παρυφίστασθαι τῇ περὶ πάντων ἐποχῇ). (*PH* 1.205)[4]

The Sceptics Sextus describes here pursue suspension of judgement as a means to tranquillity, and, though the text is not clear on this point, it is possible that they do so because they have the view that tranquillity can be achieved *only* by suspending judgement.[5] The important point for

---

[3] See also *PH* 1.232 where Sextus attributes to Arcesilaus the view that suspension of judgement is an end or goal.

[4] I follow Annas and Barnes, *Outlines*, in excising περὶ αὐτοῦ.

[5] This will turn on how we understand παρυφίστασθαι. Annas and Barnes, *Outlines*, render it by 'supervenes on', and that rendition suggests that tranquillity is dependent on suspension of judgement. I've opted for Mates's more neutral 'follows on'. Annas and Barnes, as well as Pellegrin, *Sextus Empiricus: esquisses pyrrhoniennes*, follow Mutschmann and Mau in taking καθὼς ἔμπροσθεν ὑπεμνήσαμεν to refer back to *PH* 1.29 (or, in the case of Annas and Barnes, less specifically to 1.25–9). And perhaps they do so because they take the remark at *PH* 1.29 that tranquillity follows suspension of judgement as a

my purposes, however, is that Sextus himself takes these Sceptics to represent a version of Scepticism *different from* the version he is presenting in the *Outlines*. That is why in these passages he contrasts the practices of these Sceptics with his own.[6]

Loeb also claims that 'A hallmark of Pyrrhonian skepticism is the claim that the suspension of belief is the *only* route to tranquility.'[7] But in the texts Loeb cites in support of his claim—*PH* 1.8, 1.26, 1.29, and 1.31—Sextus says that the Sceptic first experiences suspension of judgement, then tranquillity (*PH* 1.8), or that tranquillity 'followed fortuitously' (τυχικῶς παρηκολούθησεν) suspension of judgement (*PH* 1.26, 1.29), or that the Sceptics claimed that tranquillity 'follows' (ἀκολουθεῖν) suspension of judgement (*PH* 1.31). None of *those* claims is equivalent to the claim that tranquillity comes about *only* through suspension of judgement. Nonetheless, it is true that Sextus in the *Outlines* presents an argument that commits him and the Sceptic he describes to the claim that at least in *some* cases tranquillity can be achieved only through suspension of judgement. At *PH* 1.27–8 Sextus argues that anyone who believes that some things are good and other things bad will be perpetually anxious or distressed (ταράσσεται διὰ παντός).[8] If I lack something that I believe to be good, I will consider this state of affairs itself as something bad, and so be distressed by it. Yet if I succeed in acquiring something I believe to be good, I will fear the

---

shadow follows a body to be equivalent to the claim that tranquillity 'supervenes on' suspension of judgement. But it is worth noting that the word Sextus uses at *PH* 1.205 to denote what the Sceptics he is discussing there take to be the relation between suspension of judgement and tranquillity—παρυφίστασθαι—is not used by Sextus in his discussion of suspension of judgement and tranquillity at *PH* 1.25–9 (nor, if Janáček's index is reliable on this point, anywhere else in *PH*). It seems to me at least as plausible to take καθὼς ἔμπροσθεν ὑπεμνήσαμεν as a reference back to *PH* 1.30 and the remark that some Sceptics take suspension of judgement as an end or goal—especially if, with Annas and Barnes, we take the Sceptics at 1.205 to have the view that tranquillity is dependent on suspension of judgement. For someone with this view will take suspension of judgement, rather than the discovery of truth, as his goal.

  6 So, as we have seen, at *PH* 1.30 what 'some prominent Sceptics' identify as the aims or goals of Scepticism is contrasted with what 'we say' (φαμεν) they are, and at *PH* 1.203–5 what 'some' (τινες) mean when they utter the sceptical phrase 'opposed to every account there is an equal account' is contrasted with what 'I say' (εἴπω) when uttering that phrase. On these passages see also Brennan, *Ethics and Epistemology in Sextus Empiricus*, 100–2.

  7 Loeb, 'Sextus, Descartes, Hume, and Peirce: On Securing Settled Doxastic States', 218 (my emphasis).

  8 This argument recurs at *PH* 3.237–8. For a discussion of it, see especially Striker, '*Ataraxia*: Happiness as Tranquillity', 189–93, and Annas, *The Morality of Happiness*, 351–63.

loss of this good and will be anxious about doing whatever I can to prevent myself from losing it. A person can avoid the anxiety and distress associated with the pursuit and retention of things she believes to be good (as well as with the avoidance of things she believes to be bad) only by suspending judgement about whether anything is good or bad. If I do not believe about anything either that it is good or that it is bad, then I will not be distressed by the fact that I lack certain things and I will not fear the loss of anything I now possess. Call this argument *the value argument*. Now regardless of the merits of the value argument, Sextus' use of it commits him to the claim that in a range of cases— those in which a person is distressed or anxious *because* she values or disvalues something where that is a matter of believing about it either that it is good or bad—tranquillity can be achieved only through suspension of judgement. For the value argument turns on the claim that *any* belief that something is good or bad—even a true belief formed as a result of investigation on the basis of considerations that establish its truth—is a source of anxiety and distress.

The value argument, and its central claim that the belief that something is good or bad is a source of anxiety and distress, is very much like a piece of dogmatism. To that considerable extent it is in tension with Scepticism as Sextus describes it in the *Outlines*. It is worth emphasizing, however, that given certain assumptions—assumptions Sextus makes or exploits—the scope of the value argument is limited. For suppose that there are other sources of distress and anxiety besides the belief that something is good or bad, and suppose further that at least some of *these* sources of distress and anxiety are eliminable features of the human condition. The value argument does not provide the Sceptic with any reason to pursue suspension of judgement rather than the discovery of truth as the means to eliminating these other, eliminable sources of distress and anxiety. If this is right, then the value argument does not commit Sextus to the claim that in all, or even most, cases tranquillity can be achieved only through suspension of judgement. It might seem awkward for Sextus that the Sceptic in some or even most, but not all, cases pursues tranquillity by way of pursuing the discovery of truth, and I think it is. I argue below that Sextus has a good reason to discard the value argument.

On the line of interpretation I have been considering, the Sceptic replaces the discovery of truth with suspension of judgement as the means to achieving tranquillity. If this is so, however, it is difficult to see the Sceptic as someone who is engaged in philosophical investigation.

For anyone so engaged aims to discover the truth—that is, she takes the discovery of truth to be one of her objectives even if it is not her ultimate objective. For this reason some commentators have argued that once the Sceptic replaces the discovery of truth with suspension of judgement as the means to achieving tranquillity, he is no longer engaged in philosophical investigation. In two important passages from the first book of the *Outlines* Sextus describes the experience in virtue of which someone who is *not* a Sceptic *becomes* a Sceptic:

> The causal principle of scepticism we say is the hope of becoming tranquil. Men of talent, troubled by the anomaly in things and perplexed as to which of them they should rather assent to, came to investigate what in things is true and what false, thinking that by deciding these issues they would become tranquil. (*PH* 1.12)

> For having begun to do philosophy (ἀρξάμενος φιλοσοφεῖν) in order to decide among appearances and apprehend which are true and which false, so as to become tranquil, the Sceptic came upon equipollent dispute, and being unable to decide it, he suspended judgement. And when he suspended judgement, tranquillity in matters of opinion followed fortuitously. (*PH* 1.26)

Sextus presumably attributes the experience he describes here both to the very first or original Sceptics and to anyone who subsequently adopts Scepticism as a way of life. In discussing these passages Gisela Striker claims that 'when he finds himself unable to discover the truth, but nevertheless relieved of his worries once he has given up the project, the Sceptic also loses interest in the investigation of philosophical problems'.[9] On Striker's view, giving up those investigations in which

---

[9] Striker, 'Scepticism as a Kind of Philosophy', 117–18. A similar view can be found in Burnyeat, 'Can the Sceptic Live his Scepticism?', 41; Sedley, 'The Motivation of Greek Skepticism', 21; Bett, *Pyrrho, his Antecedents, and his Legacy*, 200–21; Palmer, 'Skeptical Investigation', 369, and, perhaps, Morrison, 'The Ancient Sceptic's Way of Life', 218 (who writes that the Pyrrhonist's suspension of judgement is a matter of being 'in ignorance, but absolved from the responsibility of striving for knowledge by the thoroughgoing blockage of inquiry provided by sceptical training'). In commenting on *PH* 1.7—where Sextus explains that the Sceptical way of life is called 'suspensive' (ἐφεκτική) 'from the condition that comes about in the inquirer *after the investigation*' (ἀπὸ τοῦ μετὰ τὴν ζήτησιν περὶ τὸν σκεπτόμενον γινομένου πάθους)—Janáček, *Sextus Empiricus' Sceptical Methods*, 29 writes that 'The main thing is the denial of ἐπιμονὴ ζητήσεως. The ζήτησις lapses and is replaced by the genuine sceptical ἐποχή.' Janáček's view here is endorsed by Brunschwig, 'The ὅσον ἐπὶ τῷ λόγῳ Formula in Sextus Empiricus', 244 n. 5. But it seems to me that Mates, *The Skeptic Way*, 226 is right in claiming that *PH* 1.2–3 (where the Sceptic is said to be still investigating) and *PH* 1.7 'are consistent if the phrase μετὰ τὴν ζήτησιν in 7 means in effect "after some searching"; certainly some searching is required to bring the Skeptic into a state of *aporia* and from there to *epochē*, but there seems to be no reason why, just because he is withholding assent, he must close his mind to all further consideration of the matter in question.'

one is engaged is just part of what it is to become a Sceptic—that is, to become someone who can achieve tranquillity through suspension of judgement. For Striker appears to think that once the Sceptic suspends judgement about some matter, he will no longer be distressed by the fact that he does not know the truth about that matter. And, if this is so, the Sceptic no longer has a reason to investigate the matter. Referring to *PH* 1.12, but apparently intending to refer to *PH* 1.26 as well, Striker claims that 'here we are told that a Pyrrhonist philosopher is interested in finding the truth *only* as a way of reaching peace of mind'.[10] But we are told no such thing in either passage. Sextus tells us that the Sceptic engaged in the search for the truth in order to achieve tranquillity, but that claim is neither equivalent to nor entails that the Sceptic engaged in the search for the truth *only* to achieve tranquillity. Nothing Sextus says in either passage rules out the possibility that the Sceptic engages in the search for truth *both* for its own sake *and* for the sake of tranquillity.

But is it really possible for the Sceptic (or anyone else) to set as ends for himself both tranquillity and the discovery of truth, and to pursue the latter end both for its own sake and also for the sake of the former end? Several worries might arise here. The first worry is that the ends of tranquillity and the discovery of truth are not necessarily jointly achievable. For it is possible, even likely, that there are circumstances in which the discovery of the truth about a matter will distress one and so make one less tranquil. These are circumstances in which it is not possible *both* to achieve tranquillity *and* to discover the truth, and so they are circumstances in which it is not possible to achieve tranquillity *by means of* discovering the truth. (Sextus himself, as we have seen, is committed by his use of the value argument to the claim that there are circumstances of this sort. For according to the value argument it is not possible to achieve tranquillity by discovering about something either that it is good or that it is bad.) Even if this is so, however, it does *not* follow that it is not possible to pursue both ends and to pursue one end as a means to the other end. For, of course, one may not know that in these circumstances the ends of tranquillity and the discovery of truth are not jointly achievable, and so one may not know that one cannot achieve one end (tranquillity) by achieving the other end (the discovery of truth). Moreover, even if one does know that tranquillity and the discovery of the truth about a matter are not jointly achievable, it is still possible, and perhaps even rational, for one to pursue both ends as

---

[10] Striker, 'Scepticism as a Kind of Philosophy', 117, my emphasis.

the best strategy for achieving one of them. Now, obviously, someone who knows that tranquillity and the discovery of the truth about a matter are not jointly achievable cannot, on pain of inconsistency, pursue these ends *as* jointly achievable. Hence, he cannot pursue one end as the means to the other end. Yet even if there are, or could be, circumstances in which it is not possible for one to pursue both tranquillity and the discovery of the truth about a matter as jointly achievable, it does not follow that there are no circumstances in which it is possible to pursue both of these ends as jointly achievable. If the Sceptic (or anyone else) believes, or at least does not deny, that tranquillity and the discovery of the truth about a matter are jointly achievable, and if he believes, or at least does not deny, that tranquillity can be achieved by means of discovering the truth, then the Sceptic can pursue both tranquillity and the discovery of truth and can pursue the latter end as a means to the former end.

A second worry is that the discovery of truth cannot be a subordinate end—it cannot be an end whose value is dependent on its being instrumental to, or at least consistent with, the achievement of some other end. The thought here is that someone genuinely engaged in the search for the truth about a matter wants to discover the truth about that matter regardless of the consequences this discovery might have for her pursuit of other ends—regardless, in particular, of whether she is less tranquil or happy as a result of this discovery. But I confess I cannot think of any reason why we should find this thought compelling. It seems not only possible, but a more or less common practice, to treat the discovery of the truth about a matter either as having purely instrumental value or as having both intrinsic *and* instrumental value. A medical researcher, for example, might investigate the molecular structure of a compound simply because he believes that discovering the truth about the molecular structure of the compound will help to develop a new therapy. Here he treats the value of the truth he is trying to discover as purely instrumental. If he ceases to believe that truths about the molecular structure of the compound he is investigating will, or at least might, help to develop a new therapy, he will terminate his investigation. But, alternatively, the medical researcher might *also* be interested in the truth about the molecular structure of the compound for its own sake—he might just find such matters fascinating. Now *if* the Sceptic has an interest in the truth that is independent of his pursuit of tranquillity, and so *if* the Sceptic's interest in truth is instrumental but not merely instrumental—and this is a proviso for whose truth I have not yet argued—then even when he suspends judgement about a matter and is no longer distressed by the fact that he does not know the truth about that matter, he still has a reason to investigate it.

Striker and other commentators appeal also to the following (famous) passage in support of their claim that the Sceptic achieves tranquillity by giving up the search for truth.[11]

A story told of the painter Apelles applies to the Sceptics. They say that he was painting a horse and wanted to represent in his picture the lather on the horse's mouth; but he was so unsuccessful that he gave up, took the sponge on which he had been wiping off the colors from his brush, and flung it at the picture. And when it hit the picture, it produced a representation of the horse's lather. Now the Sceptics, then, were hoping to acquire tranquillity by deciding the anomalies in what appears and is thought of, and being unable to do this they suspended judgment. But when they suspended judgment, tranquillity followed as it were fortuitously, as a shadow follows a body. (*PH* 1.28–9)

It is far from obvious just how we should formulate the moral of the Apelles story. Apelles has a certain objective (representing the lather on the horse's mouth), he is unable to achieve his objective in one way (painting the lather on the horse's mouth with his brush), and as a result he does something else by which he does *not* expect to achieve his objective (throwing the sponge on which he wiped his brush at the painting) but by which nonetheless he *does* achieve it. The Sceptic, in turn, has a certain objective (tranquillity), he is unable to achieve his objective in one way (by discovering the truth), and as a result he does something else by which he does *not* expect to achieve his objective (suspend judgement) but by which nonetheless he *does* achieve it. If, therefore, the Apelles story is supposed to reveal something about the relation between the Sceptic's suspension of judgement and his tranquillity, it is that the Sceptic does not suspend judgement in order to achieve tranquillity (just as Apelles did not throw his sponge at the painting in order to produce a representation of the lather on the horse's mouth). But in fact it may be that the moral of the Apelles story, whatever exactly it is, is supposed to apply only to the person described at *PH* 1.26 as undergoing the experience in virtue of which he *becomes* a Sceptic. That is, it may be that the Apelles story is not supposed to tell us anything about the relation between suspension of judgement and tranquillity in the case of the person who is *already* a Sceptic.

[11] See Striker, '*Ataraxia*: Happiness as Tranquillity', 192 and 'Scepticism as a Kind of Philosophy', 118; see also Bett, *Pyrrho, his Antecedents, and his Legacy*, 109.

More importantly, I do not think that the Apelles story supports the claim that the Sceptic achieves tranquillity by giving up the search for truth. Sextus does not say here that the Sceptic gives up the search for truth, but only that being unable to discover the truth, the Sceptic suspends judgement. But in reporting that he is unable to discover the truth, the Sceptic is *not* making the negative dogmatic claim that the truth cannot be known. It is true that, according to Sextus, Apelles was so unsuccessful in painting the lather on the horse's mouth that he gave up his efforts to do so (οὕτως ἀπετύγχανεν ὡς ἀπειπεῖν), and it might appear that we are supposed to conclude from this fact that the Sceptic, too, is so unsuccessful in his search for truth that he gives up that search. But I think this appearance must be misleading. For the Sceptic cannot give up the search for truth because he accepts the negative dogmatic thesis that the truth cannot be known (as Apelles might give up his efforts to paint the lather on the horse's mouth because he is convinced it cannot be done). If the Sceptic suspends judgement about whether *p*, he does so because it appears to him that the considerations he has identified in support of the truth of *p* are equally balanced by the considerations he has identified in support of the truth of its negation. If there is an analogue for the Sceptic to Apelles giving up his efforts to paint the lather on the horse's mouth, it is this: in suspending judgement about whether *p*, the Sceptic gives up the search for the truth about this matter as far as those considerations he has surveyed up to now go which bear on the question whether *p* is the case. But that simply means that for the Sceptic the search for truth now consists in looking for, and evaluating, *additional* considerations in support of the truth either of *p* or of its negation.

Two other texts in the *Outlines* have seemed to some commentators to be especially problematic for the view that the Sceptic is engaged in the search for truth. At *PH* 1.8 Sextus writes that Scepticism (Σκέψις) is 'an ability (δύναμις) to set out oppositions among things which appear and are thought of in any way at all, an ability by which, because of the equipollence (ἰσοσθένεια) in the opposed propositions and accounts, we come first to suspension of judgement (ἐποχή) and afterwards to tranquillity (ἀταραξία).' The problem is that here Sextus appears to describe the ability that is constitutive of Scepticism in such a way that the exercise of that ability eliminates any possibility that the Sceptic's investigations will end in the discovery of truth rather than suspension of judgement.[12] And the claim that it is not possible, given the Sceptic's

---

[12] Palmer, 'Skeptical Investigation', 351–2.

ability, for an investigation to end in the discovery of truth is just a version of the negative dogmatist's thesis that the truth about the matters investigated by the Sceptic cannot be known. Since, however, Sextus explicitly claims that Scepticism is *not* a form of negative dogmatism, we should try to read Sextus' description here of the ability that is constitutive of Scepticism in such a way that the exercise of that ability does not commit the Sceptic to negative dogmatism.

It is reasonable, therefore, to construe Sextus' remarks at *PH* 1.8 along the following lines. Given any candidate for belief *p*, the Sceptic is described as someone who is able to identify a conflicting candidate for belief *q* (where *q* is or entails the negation of *p*) *and* to offer an argument that purports to show that there is no reason to believe *p* rather than *q*, and vice versa. On each occasion in the past when the Sceptic has set up a conflict of this sort it has appeared to him, given the arguments he has marshalled, that he has no reason to believe *p* rather than *q*, and vice versa, and he has suspended judgement about whether *p*. And it would be unsurprising, at the very least, if it also *appears* to the Sceptic now that his future investigations, in which he exercises the same ability he has exercised in the past, will result in suspension of judgement. Nonetheless, the Sceptic does not *believe* that all of his investigations will or must result in suspension of judgement. That is why the Sceptic is not a negative dogmatist who believes that the truth cannot be known. Of course, the Sceptic need not, and does not, believe that his future investigations can and will result in the discovery of truth. The Sceptic suspends judgement about whether the truth can be known or discovered and so about whether investigation, understood as the search for truth, can succeed. But the fact that the Sceptic suspends judgement about this matter does not prevent him from undertaking an investigation and searching for the truth. It is *not* a necessary condition on engagement in the search for truth that one believe that it is possible to discover the truth. All that is required is that one not deny, as the negative dogmatist does, that it is possible to do so.

PH 1.33–4 is a second problematic text. There Sextus writes that

when someone propounds to us an argument we cannot refute, we say to him: 'Before the founder of the school to which you adhere was born, the argument of the school did not yet appear sound, but it was there in nature. In the same way, it is possible that the argument opposing the one you have just propounded is really there in nature but does not yet appear to us; so we should not yet assent to what is now thought to be a powerful argument.

The problem here is that the Sceptic can deploy this argument—call it *the possibility argument*—whenever he is presented with an argument that appears sound to him and against which he cannot raise any other objection or counter-argument.[13] And, crucially, *if* it appears to the Sceptic that the possibility argument balances out any argument against which it is directed, then he will never be in a position in which an argument appears sound to him in a way that will lead him to accept the conclusion of that argument as true. Given the availability of the possibility argument and given what the Sceptic takes to be its force, his investigation cannot end in anything but suspension of judgement.[14] Now it would be foolish to deny that Sextus' text can be read in this way, but I think another, deflationary reading is plausible as well. In presenting the possibility argument Sextus is indicating that he does not want to deny the possibility that some Sceptics (or, for that matter, some non-Sceptics) will find the argument persuasive. At the same time, however, Sextus can concede that it is possible that some Sceptics will *not* find the possibility argument persuasive. The passage at *PH* 1.33–4 does not require, as far as I can see, that according to Sextus *every* Sceptic will find the possibility argument as persuasive as any argument against which it is deployed. So for all Sextus has said in this passage the mere availability of the possibility argument does not guarantee that in every case the Sceptic's investigation will end in suspension of judgement.

To this point I have been arguing that none of the texts commonly cited in support of the view that the Sceptic is not engaged in the search for truth needs to be read in that way. But these exegetical arguments leave unanswered the question *why* the Sceptic—that is, someone who is able to achieve tranquillity by suspending judgement—engages in the search for truth. There is a genuine puzzle here, and I think it arises in several ways.

Consider, first, the case in which the Sceptic is distressed by the fact that he does not know whether *p* where the value of *p* is such that the Sceptic has not previously considered or investigated, and so has not previously suspended judgement about, whether *p* is the case. Given that in the past his investigations have led him to suspend judgement, it appears to the Sceptic that if he were to investigate whether *p* is the case,

---

[13] Versions of the possibility argument are presented by Sextus at *PH* 1.89, 1.96, 1.143, 2.40, and 3.233–4.

[14] Cf. Palmer, 'Skeptical Investigation', 356, and Striker, 'Scepticism as a Kind of Philosophy', 127–8. The possibility argument has at least one champion in Hankinson, *The Sceptics*, 30.

this investigation, too, would lead him to suspend judgement. Moreover, given that in the past he has achieved tranquillity by suspending judgement, it appears to the Sceptic that if he were to suspend judgement about whether p, he would achieve tranquillity, that is, he would no longer be distressed, as he now is, by the fact that he does not know whether p. The puzzle, then, is why in this case the Sceptic doesn't pursue suspension of judgement rather than the discovery of truth as the means to tranquillity. The solution to this puzzle cannot be that if the Sceptic were to do so, he would thereby commit himself to a form of negative dogmatism. The Sceptic can pursue suspension of judgement as a means to tranquillity without denying either that it is possible to discover the truth or that it is possible to achieve tranquillity by discovering the truth. It will just appear to him, as a result of his past experience, that he can achieve tranquillity by suspending judgement at least as easily as he can by discovering the truth. I argued earlier that the Sceptic cannot pursue suspension of judgement rather than the discovery of truth as a means to tranquillity on the grounds that it is not possible to discover the truth. The point here is simply that the Sceptic's pursuit of suspension of judgement as a means to tranquillity need not be based in this way on negative dogmatism.

Consider next the case in which the Sceptic investigates whether p is the case. The Sceptic does so, according to Sextus, in order to achieve tranquillity. The Sceptic is distressed and the source of his distress is, as it appears to him, the fact that he does not know whether p. Since this is so he attempts to eliminate the distress he feels by acquiring the relevant bit of knowledge he lacks, that is, by discovering whether or not p is the case. But, as it happens, the Sceptic's investigation leads him to suspend judgement about whether p; and, again, as it happens, once the Sceptic suspends judgement about whether p he is no longer distressed by the fact that he does not know whether p. If this is so, however, the Sceptic has now lost his original reason for investigating whether p is the case. For he has achieved, by other means, the tranquillity he sought to achieve through his investigation and its termination in the discovery of truth. Yet if the Sceptic has lost his original reason for investigating whether p is the case, what reason does he have to continue this investigation? And if he has no reason to do so, how can the Sceptic plausibly claim, as Sextus does on the Sceptic's behalf, that he is *still* investigating (*PH* 1.2)? The quick answer to these questions is that the Sceptic's suspension of judgement is, and is understood by him to be, provisional. That is why Sextus occasionally remarks that the Sceptic's suspension of judgement obtains only as far as an argument or set of considerations go (ὅσον ἐπὶ τῷ λόγῳ) or 'up to now' (μέχρι or ἄχρι νῦν).[15] It is also the reason why when the Sceptic utters one of the sceptical phrases catalogued at *PH* 1.187–205, his utterance is governed at least implicitly by a temporal qualifier.[16] The Sceptic's suspension of judgement can be disturbed or unsettled by the introduction of a new consideration that bears on the matter about which he has suspended judgement. The Sceptic will wonder whether this new consideration establishes the truth of p (or of its negation), and he will be distressed by the fact that he does not know whether it does. And to be distressed by *this* fact is just to be distressed again by the fact that one doesn't know whether p. This distress, or rather the desire to eliminate it, provides the Sceptic with his reason to continue investigating the matter.

This quick answer, however, comes at the price of generating in a second way the same puzzle. Given his past experience it appears to the Sceptic that continued investigation of whether p is the case will result in suspension of judgement. Moreover, and again given his past experience, it appears to him that by suspending judgement about whether p he will eliminate the distress he feels once again because he does not know whether p. Why, then, doesn't the Sceptic pursue suspension of judgement rather than the discovery of truth as the means to restoring the tranquillity he has lost?

One possible solution to this puzzle is that for the Sceptic suspension of judgement is not something that can be achieved by pursuing it directly.[17] The problem here is that it is not clear how we are to understand the claim that, according to Sextus, it is not possible to pursue suspension of judgement *directly*. It is clear that Sextus does not think that the Sceptic (or anyone else) can suspend judgement simply by deciding or intending to do so. For if the Sceptic could suspend judgement in this way, he would not need to seek or devise, as he does, arguments for and against the truth of the candidate for belief that is under consideration. These arguments are supposed to put the Sceptic in a position in which it appears to him that for the relevant value of p there is no reason to believe either p or its negation. Suspension of judgement is

[15] As Barnes, *The Toils of Scepticism*, 10, has noted, citing *PH* 1.25, 1.200, 1.201, and 3.70.

[16] See also *PH* 1.193 (νῦν), 1.197 (οὕτω πέπονθα νῦν), 1.200 (ἄχρι νῦν), 1.201 (πρὸς τὸ παρόν). Contrast Palmer, 'Skeptical Investigation', 372.

[17] This sort of view is suggested by some remarks in Annas, 'Scepticism Old and New', 242 and n. 14.

the Sceptic's *response* to finding himself in this position. Moreover—and this is an issue I examine in Chapter 2—this position is one that, according to Sextus, in some sense *requires* or *necessitates* suspension of judgement. But it does not follow from the fact that the Sceptic cannot suspend judgement simply by deciding or intending to do so that the Sceptic cannot explicitly *aim* to suspend judgement. For the Sceptic can explicitly aim to suspend judgement by explicitly aiming to put himself in a position in which for the relevant value of *p* it appears to him that there is no reason to believe either *p* or its negation. And he can explicitly aim to do *this* by explicitly aiming, as he does, to seek or devise arguments for and against the truth of *p*. Yet if the Sceptic can explicitly aim to suspend judgement, then he can explicitly aim to suspend judgement as a means to achieving tranquillity.

So, on the one hand, the claim that the Sceptic cannot pursue suspension of judgement directly is true if it is understood as the claim that the Sceptic cannot suspend judgement simply by deciding or intending to do so. But the truth of *this* claim cannot explain why the Sceptic pursues the discovery of truth rather than suspension of judgement as a means to tranquillity. For, of course, it is also true that the Sceptic cannot discover the truth simply by deciding or intending to do so. On the other hand, the claim that the Sceptic cannot pursue suspension of judgement directly is false if it is understood as the claim that the Sceptic cannot explicitly aim to suspend judgement. Now, according to Sextus, the Sceptic does *not* explicitly aim to suspend judgement, and so he does not explicitly aim to suspend judgement as a means to achieving tranquillity. This is one thing that distinguishes the Sceptic, as Sextus describes him, from other figures in the history of ancient scepticism like Timon and Aenesidemus. The question I am pressing is *why*, according to Sextus, the Sceptic does not pursue suspension of judgement, or aim explicitly to suspend judgement, as a means to tranquillity.

Notice, first, that the Sceptic will pursue suspension of judgement rather than the discovery of truth as a means to tranquillity *only if* the Sceptic is interested in the discovery of truth *merely* as a means to tranquillity. To see that this is so suppose that the Sceptic can achieve tranquillity either by discovering the truth or by suspending judgement, and that the Sceptic is interested in the discovery of truth for its own sake and not merely as a means to tranquillity. Since the Sceptic has an interest in the discovery of truth for its own sake, and lacks any such interest in suspension of judgement, he has a reason to prefer the discovery of truth to suspension of judgement as a means to tranquillity. So the Sceptic will pursue tranquillity by way of suspension of judgement only if he lacks an interest in the discovery of truth for its own sake and, consequently, has no reason to prefer the discovery of truth to suspension of judgement as a means to tranquillity. But—and this is the important point—if the Sceptic lacks an interest in the discovery of truth for its own sake, and so if he is interested in it merely as a means to tranquillity, then the Sceptic *also* lacks the motive that Sextus attributes to him for seeking tranquillity in the first place.

Sextus tells us that the Sceptic seeks tranquillity because he is distressed, and the Sceptic is distressed because for some value of *p* he does not know whether *p* is the case (*PH* 1.12, 1.26). If this is so, it follows, first, that the Sceptic has an interest in knowing whether *p* where this interest is, at least in part, a desire to know whether *p*. The Sceptic is distressed by his failure to know whether *p* because his desire to know whether *p* is unsatisfied and an unsatisfied desire is, to one degree or another, a source of distress. If the Sceptic were indifferent to knowing whether *p*—that is, if he did not care about knowing whether *p* and had no desire to know whether *p*—he would not be distressed, as Sextus says he is, by the fact that he does not know whether *p*. Second, the Sceptic's interest in knowing whether *p* cannot be an interest in this knowledge *as a means to tranquillity*. This is so because the Sceptic's interest in knowing whether *p*, together with the fact that he does not know whether *p*, is supposed to be the source of the distress that, in turn, is the source of the desire to alleviate it. And *this* desire just is a desire for tranquillity. So the Sceptic's interest in knowing whether *p* cannot presuppose the very desire for tranquillity for which it is ultimately the source. According to Sextus the Sceptic is distressed, and so motivated to seek tranquillity, precisely because he has an interest in the discovery of truth that is *not* an interest in it as a means to tranquillity. If the Sceptic lacked an interest of this sort in the discovery of truth, he would be immune to just the kind of distress that, Sextus says, motivates him to seek tranquillity. In this way Sextus' account of why the Sceptic seeks tranquillity is coherent only if the Sceptic has an interest in the discovery of truth for its own sake, that is, independently of any instrumental relation it bears to tranquillity. That interest, in turn, gives the Sceptic a reason to pursue the discovery of truth rather than suspension of judgement as a means to tranquillity.

This line of thought makes it clear why the value argument (*PH* 1.27–8) is a problem for Sextus. The source of distress Sextus identifies there is not—as we might have expected from Sextus' remarks at *PH* 1.12 and 1.26—the fact that one does not know whether something is good or bad. It is, rather, any *belief* one has that something is good or bad.

But if *any* belief about the goodness or badness of something is a source of distress, then discovering the truth about the value of something is an obstacle, not a means, to tranquillity. For, obviously, to discover the truth about the value of something is to come to know, and hence to believe, either that it is good or that it is bad. So, on the one hand, Sextus claims at *PH* 1.12 and 1.26 that the Sceptic is distressed by his failure to know certain things. This claim is intelligible only if the Sceptic has an interest in the discovery of truth for its own sake and not merely as a means to tranquillity. This interest gives the Sceptic a reason to pursue the discovery of truth rather than suspension of judgement as a means to tranquillity. But, on the other hand, the value argument and its central claim that any belief about the goodness or badness of something is a source of distress requires the Sceptic to disregard his interest in the discovery of truth and to pursue suspension of judgement as a means to tranquillity.

Consider next a passage early in the second book of the *Outlines* where Sextus is responding to the charge that the Sceptic cannot investigate (or even think about) those matters about which the dogmatic philosopher holds beliefs. At *PH* 2.11 Sextus writes:

Consider whether even now the dogmatists are not precluded from investigation. For those who agree that they do not know how objects are in their nature it is not inconsistent (οὐ... ἀνακόλουθον) to investigate them; but for those who think they know them accurately, it is. For the latter [i.e. the dogmatists] the investigation is already at its end, as they suppose, but for the former, the reason why any investigation is undertaken—the thought that they have not made a discovery—is still present (δι' ὃ πᾶσα συνίσταται ζήτησις ἀκμὴν ὑπάρχει, τὸ νομίζειν ὡς οὐχ εὑρήκασιν).

Sextus claims here that *anyone*, the Sceptic included, who investigates a matter does so because he does not know, and so has not yet discovered, the truth about that matter. But the fact that I do not know whether *p* can explain why I am investigating the matter *only if*, first, I desire to know whether *p*, and, second, I believe or at least do not deny that it is possible to discover, and so to know, whether *p*. If I have no desire to know whether *p*, or if I deny that it is possible to know whether *p*, then the fact that I do not know whether *p* will not motivate me to investigate whether *p*. Ignorance is a motive for investigation only in conjunction with a desire to know and, at a minimum, an open mind about the possibility of knowledge. So in this passage Sextus, at least by implication, attributes to the Sceptic a desire to know the truth about any matter he investigates. This desire is a reason for the Sceptic to pursue the discovery of truth rather than suspension of judgement as a means to tranquillity provided that the Sceptic believes, or at least does not deny, that tranquillity can be achieved by means of discovering the truth. I have already argued that the Sceptic is not in a position to deny that it is possible to achieve tranquillity by discovering the truth. If this is right, then the Sceptic will pursue both the discovery of truth and tranquillity, but he will not pursue the discovery of truth *merely* as a means to tranquillity.[18]

So the passage at *PH* 2.11 suggests the following solution to our puzzle. When the Sceptic is initially distressed by the fact that he does not know whether *p* is the case, or when he has suspended judgement about the matter but is once again distressed by the fact that he does not know whether *p*, he pursues the discovery of truth rather than suspension of judgement as the means to tranquillity. The Sceptic does so because he has an interest in discovering whether *p* that is independent of any contribution this discovery makes to the achievement of tranquillity. For the Sceptic as Sextus describes him the discovery of truth, unlike suspension of judgement, is not merely a means to an end. The fact that the Sceptic pursues the discovery of truth as an end in itself does not mean that he pursues the discovery of truth as his *ultimate* end. For, of course, the Sceptic pursues the discovery of truth not only as an end in itself but also as a means to something else. Tranquillity, not the discovery of truth, is the Sceptic's ultimate end. In describing Scepticism

---

[18] Palmer, 'Skeptical Investigation', 368–9, claims that the passage at *PH* 2.11 can be read 'as a purely *ad hominem* point against the dogmatists who claim that the Skeptic is precluded from inquiring into their own theories: given that *they* conceive of the goal of inquiry as the discovery of truth, then a necessary condition of being able to conduct an inquiry of the type they pursue is the belief that one does not already know the truth, so their complaint against the Skeptic backfires since they suppose that they are already in possession of the truth.' But, first, Palmer does not explain why it is a point against the dogmatist who believes that *p* that he is not *still* investigating or cannot (without giving up his belief that *p*) investigate whether *p* is the case. It is, after all, the Sceptic, not the dogmatist, who claims both that he is *still* investigating and that investigation is a constitutive feature of his way of life. Second, Palmer can read *PH* 2.11 in the way he describes only by ignoring, as he does, the crucial portion of the text: Sextus explicitly says that those who agree that they do not know what the nature of a given object is—i.e. the Sceptics—have *as their reason for engaging in any investigation* the fact that they think they have not discovered what the nature of that object is.

as having an ultimate end, Sextus simply employs without endorsing the standard dogmatic philosophical definitions of the ultimate end (*PH* 1.25). Tranquillity alone satisfies those definitions. For tranquillity alone is that for the sake of which everything else, the discovery of truth included, is pursued while it itself is not pursued for the sake of anything else.

I now want to turn to a second puzzle about whether and how the Sceptic's use of certain arguments is compatible with the search for truth. At *PH* 1.164–9 Sextus introduces a set of five modes or argument forms—the so-called Agrippan modes—that lead, either individually or in combination with one another, to suspension of judgement.[19] The Agrippan modes purport to show that for some value of *p* there is an undecided disagreement over whether *p* (the mode from disagreement), or that the attempt to establish the truth of *p* relies on mere assertion (the mode from hypothesis) or involves reasoning in a circle (the reciprocal mode) or generates an infinite regress (the mode from infinite regress). Some commentators have claimed that in purporting to show this the Agrippan modes purport to show, and are taken by the Sceptic to show, that for any value of *p* to which they apply, there is not and cannot be a reason to believe that *p*. But *this* conclusion is simply the negative dogmatic thesis that for a range of values for *p*—those to which the Agrippan modes apply—it is not possible to know whether *p*. The puzzle, then, is how the Sceptic can be engaged in the search for the truth about some matter while using, as he does, arguments that have as their conclusion, and are taken by the Sceptic to have as their conclusion, that the truth about this matter cannot be known. Genuine engagement in the search for truth requires at a minimum that one does not deny that it is possible to discover the truth for which one is searching. But insofar as he uses the Agrippan modes the Sceptic effectively denies that it is possible to discover the truth for which he is searching. Moreover, as commentators regularly observe, Sextus writes that 'it is possible to refer every object of investigation to these modes' (πᾶν τὸ ζητούμενον εἰς τούτους ἀνάγειν τοὺς τρόπους ἐνδέχεται, *PH* 1.169). If, as Sextus claims here, the Agrippan modes have universal application, then the Sceptic has arguments that purport to show, and

---

[19] Sextus reports that these modes of suspension of judgement were devised by 'the more recent sceptics' (οἱ νεώτεροι Σκεπτικοί) in contrast to 'the older sceptics' (οἱ ἀρχαιότεροι Σκεπτικοί) who are said at *PH* 1.36 to have handed down the ten modes of suspension of judgement and who include, as Sextus indicates elsewhere (*M* 7.345), Aenesidemus. Diogenes Laertius (9.88) attributes the five modes to Agrippa.

are taken by the Sceptic to show, that *no* investigation can succeed—that *no* truth for which one might search can be discovered. But how can someone who has at his disposal, as the Sceptic does, arguments that rule out the very possibility of a successful investigation or the discovery of truth be genuinely engaged in the search for truth?[20]

There is a solution to this puzzle, and it is a solution which seems to me to be available to the Sceptic, but I want to be clear that Sextus nowhere explicitly formulates it. So I am concerned here less with exegesis and more with those possibilities that fall within the logical space of Scepticism as Sextus describes it. The solution I have in mind turns on two points. First, someone who, like the Sceptic, takes the Agrippan modes to have universal application is not *for that reason alone* committed to a general negative dogmatism. For the claim that the Agrippan modes can be applied to any matter the Sceptic investigates is *not* equivalent to the claim that the Agrippan modes can be *successfully* applied in every case. The Agrippan modes together constitute a formal, and therefore topic-neutral, argumentative strategy. But while its topic neutrality guarantees that the Agrippan strategy has universal application, it cannot by itself guarantee that every application of the strategy will be successful. So the fact that the Sceptic uses an argumentative strategy with univeral application commits him to a general negative dogmatism *only if* he *also* believes that every application of the Agrippan strategy will be successful.

The second point, then, is that the Sceptic has no reason to believe that every application of the Agrippan strategy will be successful. Here is one version of that strategy.[21] For some value of p, either the truth of p is merely asserted or it is established on the basis of some reason $R1$. If the truth of p is merely asserted, the hypothetical mode applies. According to that mode the mere assertion of p cannot establish the truth of p. For the mere assertion of p is no more or less credible than the mere assertion of its negation. If the truth of p is established on the basis of

---

[20] For versions of this objection to the Sceptic's use of the Agrippan modes, see Palmer, 'Skeptical Investigation', 356–9, and Striker, 'Scepticism as a Kind of Philosophy', 120.

[21] This version of the Agrippan strategy is developed by Barnes, *The Toils of Scepticism*, 119, but it is based on Sextus' own description at *PH* 1.178–9 of a strategy that employs three (not, as Sextus curiously says, two) of the Agrippan modes: the mode from disagreement, the reciprocal mode, and the mode from infinite regress. Barnes produces his strategy by simply replacing the mode from disagreement with the hypothetical mode. If the Sceptic's use of this strategy or one of its variants need not commit him to negative dogmatism, then his use of the Agrippan modes individually need not do so.

some reason $R1$, then $R1$ is either the same as or different from p. If $R1$ is the same as p, the reciprocal mode applies. The attempt to establish the truth of p on the basis of $R1$ involves reasoning in a (very small) circle. If $R1$ is different from p, then either the truth of $R1$ is merely asserted or it is established on the basis of a reason $R2$. If $R1$ is merely asserted, the hypothetical mode applies. If the truth of $R1$ is established on the basis of $R2$, then either $R2$ is the same as or different from $R1$. If $R2$ is the same as $R1$ (or p), the reciprocal mode applies. If $R2$ is different from $R1$, then either the truth of $R2$ is merely asserted or it is established on the basis of a reason $R3$; and so on. The effort to establish the truth of p on the basis of a reason generates an infinite sequence of reasons, and the mode from infinite regress applies. According to this mode an infinite sequence of reasons cannot establish the truth of p.[22]

The crux of the Agrippan strategy is (1) the demand, given any reason R that is offered as establishing the truth of p, for an *additional* reason that establishes the truth of R, and (2) the rejection as mere assertion of any reason whose truth is not established by another reason. The question, however, is why the Sceptic would believe that for *any* reason R that is offered as establishing, either directly or indirectly, the truth of p, it is reasonable or even intelligible to demand an additional reason that establishes the truth of R. If R is a reason whose truth is self-evident, then someone who offers R as establishing the truth of p, and does so without offering an additional reason that establishes the truth of R, is not merely asserting R. For the charge of mere assertion, and so the hypothetical mode, can be successfully applied only to a reason whose truth is not self-evident and must be established by some additional reason. And if $R1$ is different from p—as it must be if its truth is self-evident—then the reciprocal mode cannot be successfully applied to someone who offers R as establishing the truth of p. And, finally, if someone who offers R as establishing the truth of p is not merely asserting R and is not reasoning in a circle, then there is no need for him to offer an additional reason that establishes the truth of R. Yet if he does not offer an additional reason as establishing the truth of R, then the mode from infinite regress does not apply.

Call a reason whose truth is self-evident a *basic reason*.[23] Every application of the Agrippan strategy will be successful *only if* there are

---

[22] See Barnes, *The Toils of Scepticism*, 44–8 on why this is so or why the Sceptic takes this to be so.

[23] Ibid. 122–37 sketches an 'externalist' account of basic beliefs or items of knowledge to which the dogmatic philosopher can appeal in response to the Agrippan strategy, and

not and cannot be basic reasons. More importantly, the Sceptic believes that every application of the Agrippan strategy will be successful *only if* he believes that there are not and cannot be basic reasons. So the Sceptic's use of the Agrippan strategy commits him to a general negative dogmatism (the general view that nothing can be known or discovered) *only if* the Sceptic is also, and independently, committed to a negative dogmatism about basic reasons (the view that there are not and cannot be basic reasons). But the Sceptic has no reason to believe that there are not and cannot be basic reasons, and he will suspend judgement about the matter. In this connection two points are important.

First, for any proposition *p*, the Sceptic can use one or more of the Ten Modes (*PH* 1.35–163) to argue that it appears to some creature under some condition that *q* where *q* is or entails the negation of *p*. But, it might be thought, if it appears to some creature under some condition that *q*, and so that not-*p*, then the truth of *p* is not self-evident. If the truth of *p* is not self-evident, then *p* is not a basic reason. For a basic reason is a proposition whose truth *is* self-evident and whose self-evident truth establishes the truth of a proposition whose truth is not self-evident. If this is so, then in the Ten Modes the Sceptic has arguments that purport to show, and are taken by the Sceptic to show, that the truth of any proposed basic reason is *not* self-evident but must be established, if it can, by appeal to the truth of some other proposition. And if this is so, then the Sceptic has a reason to accept a negative dogmatism about basic reasons, that is, he has a reason to believe that there are not and cannot be basic reasons. This line of thought, however, turns on a confusion about what it is for the truth of a proposition to be self-evident and so what it is for something to be a basic reason. It is not the case that, in order for the truth of *p* to be self-evident, the truth of *p* must be self-evident to *any* creature under *any* condition. The truth of *p* is self-evident if and only if it is possible to know that *p* in such a way that one's knowledge that *p* is not derived from or based on some other item of knowledge one has. It can be possible to know that *p* in this way even if no creature in fact knows that *p*. The most the Ten Modes can be used to show is that even if the truth of *p* is self-evident, there are creatures who fail to know that *p* and so fail to know that *p* in the special

he attributes this account to Galen and certain Stoics. My point here, in contrast, is simply that the Sceptic has no reason to deny the possibility of what I am calling basic reasons (though he need not have any reason to accept their possibility). If the Sceptic does not deny the possibility of basic reasons, then his use of the Agrippan strategy does not commit him to a general negative dogmatism.

way in which it is possible to know something whose truth is self-evident. In this way the most the Ten Modes can be used to show is that no basic reason is universally accessible—that there is nothing whose truth is self-evident to any creature under any condition. But that fact, if it is a fact, has no bearing on the question whether there are or can be basic reasons.[24]

Second, if the Sceptic suspends judgement about the possibility of basic reasons, then he suspends judgement about whether every application of the Agrippan strategy will be successful. The fact that he suspends judgement about *this*, in turn, allows the Sceptic to use the Agrippan strategy without thereby committing himself to a general negative dogmatism. And if this is so, then the Sceptic's use of the Agrippan strategy is compatible with a genuine engagement in the search for truth.

In this chapter I have argued that, according to Sextus, the Sceptic is engaged in the search for truth, and this is so in part because for the Sceptic the discovery of truth is not merely a means to tranquillity but also an end in itself. I have also claimed that the Sceptic's use of certain arguments, including the Agrippan modes, does not by itself commit him to negative dogmatism and so is compatible with the search for truth.

Insofar as the Sceptic is engaged in the search for truth he has a certain aim, namely, to discover the truth. Yet if this is an aim the Sceptic has, it cannot be the only aim the Sceptic has. For insofar as the

---

[24] If the notion of being apprehended or known by means of itself (τὸ καταλαμβάνεσθαι ἐξ ἑαυτοῦ) is equivalent to the notion of being self-evident, then it might be thought that at *PH* 1.178 Sextus assumes that the fact that it appears to one person that *p* and to another person that not-*p* is sufficient to show that *p* cannot be known by means of itself and, therefore, is not self-evident. But it seems to me that in this passage neither Sextus nor those whose argument he is reporting make this assumption. Sextus explains that 'the more recent Sceptics' who devised the Agrippan modes also argued that the fact that nothing is known by means of itself, and therefore that nothing is self-evident, follows from the fact there is an 'undecided' (ἀνεπίκριτος) dispute among natural scientists (φυσικοί) over all objects of perception and of thought. According to this argument, then, the fact that a given proposition *p* is not known by means of itself and therefore is not self-evident does *not* follow from the fact that it appears to one creature that *p* and to another creature (or to the same creature in different circumstances) that not-*p*. The conclusion that *p* is not self-evident, according to this argument, follows only from the fact that the dispute over whether *p* is the case is 'undecided', i.e. from the fact that there is no reason to believe either *p* or its negation. And that is so, the argument continues, because any consideration that could serve as a reason to believe *p* rather than its negation, or vice versa, would itself be an object of perception or an object of thought and, for that reason, subject to the dispute it is supposed to resolve.

Sceptic aims to discover the truth, he also aims to do whatever is required in order for him (or anyone else) to discover the truth. And if this is so, then the Sceptic, as someone engaged in the search for truth, aims to satisfy those rational requirements that govern the search for truth. So, for example, the Sceptic aims to satisfy the requirement that one suspend judgement about whether p if one has no reason to believe either p or its negation. The fact that the Sceptic aims to satisfy this rational requirement can serve as the basis for a novel explanation of a significant feature of Scepticism. For Sextus reports that if it appears to the Sceptic that he has no reason to believe either p or its negation, then not only does the Sceptic suspend judgement about whether p but it is *necessary* for him to do so.[25] The consensus among commentators is that according to Sextus the necessity that characterizes the Sceptic's suspension of judgement is causal: its appearing to one that there is no reason to believe either p or its negation is related to suspension of judgement about whether p as cause to effect. That is why, and the sense in which, if it appears to the Sceptic that there is no reason to believe either p or its negation, he *must* suspend judgement about whether p. But, as I shall argue in Chapter 2, if the Sceptic is engaged in the search for truth, then it is possible to see the necessity that characterizes the Sceptic's suspension of judgement not only as causal but also, and primarily, as hypothetical. According to Sextus, I shall argue, it is necessary for the Sceptic to suspend judgement *if* he is to satisfy, as he aims to do, certain basic rational requirements.

[25] *PH* 1.61, 1.78, 1.89, 1.121, 1.128, 1.129, 1.140, 1.163, and 1.170.

2

Necessity and Rationality

Scepticism in modern philosophy is the view that knowledge or reasonable belief of one kind or another—about the physical world, the minds of others, the past, the future—is impossible.[1] Scepticism as Sextus defines it, however, is not a philosophical view but rather an ability (δύναμις) and a way of life organized around the exercise of that ability. The Sceptic is someone who is able to construct conflicts between candidates for belief in various ways (*PH* 1.8 and *PH* 1.31–4). For Sextus a conflict between two candidates for belief is a conflict between two *appearances* (φαινόμενα or φαντασίαι) that can be expressed by a pair of sentences of the form

    (1) It appears to S that p.
    (2) It appears to S^* that q.

where q is or entails the negation of p, and S and S^* designate different persons (or creatures) or the same person (or creature) in different circumstances. One way in which it can appear to me that p is by my having a perceptual experience that p, e.g. that the wine is sweet, or that the apple is red. But for Sextus the content of an appearance need not be a proposition that specifies a perceptible state of affairs. It can appear to me that an argument is valid or that pleasure is the good or that investors are irrationally exuberant.[2] Now (1) and (2) do not conflict.

---

[1] For scepticism in modern philosophy as the view that knowledge is impossible, and so, like its rivals, as a general theory of knowledge, see especially Stroud, 'Scepticism, "Externalism", and Epistemology'. Scepticism in ancient philosophy, too, is sometimes the view that knowledge is impossible. At Cicero, *Acad.* 2.148, Catulus endorses the view (which he attributes to his father, and which his father in turn attributed to Carneades) that nothing can be known (*nihil esse quod percipi posset*); and at *Acad.* 2.59 Lucullus attributes this view to both Arcesilaus and Carneades (and cf. *Acad.* 2.78). Sextus attributes the view that nothing can be known to Clitomachus, Carneades, and 'other Academics' (*PH* 1.3) as well as to the Cyrenaics (*PH* 1.215).

[2] In explicating at *PH* 1.9 the definition he offers at *PH* 1.8 of Scepticism, Sextus restricts φαινόμενα ('appearances' or, more literally, 'things that appear') to τὰ αἰσθητά where τὰ αἰσθητά are the contents of perceptual experiences, e.g. that the wine is sweet.

For (1) reports that *S* has an appearance that *p*, (2) reports that *S** has an appearance that *q*, and it is possible for both (1) and (2) to be true. Nonetheless, the appearance reported by (1) (= the appearance that *p*) conflicts with the appearance reported by (2) (= the appearance that *q*), and this is so because the proposition that serves as the content of the appearance reported by (1) (= *p*) conflicts with the proposition that serves as the content of the appearance reported by (2) (= *q*). An appearance is true just in case the proposition that serves as its content is true, and since *q* is or entails the negation of *p*, it is not possible for both the appearance that *p* and the appearance that *q* to be true. Sextus, like the dogmatic philosophers with whom he engages, conceives of a belief as something that is formed by giving assent to an appearance or, alternatively, to the proposition that serves as the content of that appearance.[3] Thus a conflict between two appearances, or between the two propositions that are the contents of these two appearances, is a conflict between two candidates for belief. And the Sceptic, according to Sextus, is someone who is able to construct conflicts of this sort.

The Sceptic is a philosopher familiar with a wide range of philosophical views, and one way in which he is able to construct a conflict between two candidates for belief about some matter is by identifying a conflict between existing philosophical views on that matter. So, for instance, Sextus notes that the views of philosophers about the number and identity of the basic material elements conflict (*PH* 3.30–2). He also observes that some philosophers believe while other philosophers like Parmenides and Melissus deny that motion exists (*PH* 3.65). But in addition to cataloguing philosophical views the Sceptic also produces philosophical arguments. In response to existing philosophical arguments for the existence of causes (αἴτια), Sextus devises a series of arguments that purport to show that there are no causes (*PH* 3.20–9).

In doing so he contrasts φαινόμενα with τὰ νοητά where τὰ νοητά are the contents of thoughts, e.g. that pleasure is the good. More frequently, however, Sextus uses φαινόμενον or the cognate noun φαντασία more broadly for any psychological state that can be described as its appearing to me that *p* where *p* need not specify a perceptible state of affairs (*PH* 1.19, 1.22). Just as it can appear to me without my believing that the wine is sweet, so I can have the thought, and in this way it can appear to me without my believing, that pleasure is the good.

[3] For my purposes here the distinction between assenting to an appearance and assenting to the propositional content of that appearance is not important. Frede, 'The Stoic Doctrine of the Affections of the Soul', 103–6 argues that for the Stoics this distinction is important, and that on their view belief is the product of assent given to an appearance (or impression) and not, or not only, to its propositional content.

He makes it clear that his purpose in doing so is not to establish that there are no causes, but to create a conflict between two candidates for belief about the existence of causes. Suppose, to take a third kind of case, it appears to some person, philosopher or non-philosopher, that *p* where the possible values for *p* range from mundane perceptual propositions (e.g. 'Grass is green', 'Honey is sweet') to propositions of morality or etiquette ('It is wrong to have sex in public'). The Sceptic can argue, in various ways codified in the Ten Modes (*PH* 1.35–163), that it appears to someone else, or to the same person in different circumstances, that *q* where *q* is or entails the negation of *p*.[4]

Given a conflict between two candidates for belief *p* and *q*, the Sceptic suspends judgement about whether *p* where doing so is a matter of withholding assent both from *p* and from *q*.[5] According to Sextus, however, suspension of judgement (ἐποχή) is the Sceptic's response not to the fact that two candidates for belief conflict, but to the fact that a conflict between two candidates for belief is, in Sextus' terminology, 'equipollent' (ἰσοσθενής). What does Sextus mean in claiming that a conflict between candidates for belief is equipollent?[6] Sextus routinely argues that a conflict between two candidates for belief is equipollent by deploying instances of one or more of the argument forms commonly referred to as the Agrippan modes. An instance of an Agrippan mode is an argument that purports to show that there is no reason to believe a candidate for belief *p* by showing that any proposed reason to believe

---

[4] In the first of the Ten Modes Sextus appeals to differences in the generation, composition, and preferences of animals as considerations that make it 'likely' (εἰκός *PH* 1.43, 1.54) that the same object appears in different and incompatible ways to animals of different species. As Annas and Barnes, *The Modes of Scepticism*, 40–1, note, this first mode concerns the way things appear to non-human animals and, as a result, Sextus does not construct actual conflicts of appearances or candidates for belief, but instead offers arguments that are supposed to show that it is likely that there are conflicts between the ways in which a given object appears to animals of different species.

[5] See *PH* 1.10 where Sextus writes that 'Suspension of judgement is a state of the intellect on account of which we neither deny nor affirm something (ἐποχὴ δέ ἐστι στάσις διανοίας δι᾿ ἣν οὔτε αἴρομέν τι οὔτε τίθεμεν).'

[6] At *PH* 1.10 Sextus defines equipollence as 'equality with respect to credibility and lack of credibility (κατὰ πίστιν καὶ ἀπιστίαν): none of the conflicting arguments take precedence over any other as being more credible (πιστότερον).' Sextus repeatedly defines '*p* and *q* are equipollent' as '*p* and *q* are equal κατὰ πίστιν καὶ ἀπιστίαν'. See *PH* 1.196, 1.198–9, 1.202–3, 1.222, 1.227, and 1.232. To my knowledge the one exception in *PH* is 1.190 where (reading Mutschmann and Mau's text with Pappenheim's supplement) Sextus writes 'By "equipollence" we mean equality in what appears plausible to us (τὴν <ἰσότητα τὴν> κατὰ τὸ φαινόμενον ἡμῖν πιθανόν).' Sextus makes reference to ἴση πιθανότης at *PH* 1.183 (where this might reflect Aenesidemus' usage) and 2.79.

p generates an infinite regress or relies on an arbitrary assumption or involves reasoning in a circle. Since the Sceptic takes instances of the Agrippan modes to have this force and deploys them to establish that a conflict between candidates for belief is equipollent, a conflict between two candidates for belief *p* and *q* is equipollent for the Sceptic if and only if it appears to him that there is no reason to believe either *p* or *q*.[7] Now two candidates for belief *p* and *q* conflict just in case *q* is or entails the negation of *p*. So if it appears to the Sceptic that there is no reason to believe either *p* or *q*, then it appears to him that there is no reason to believe either *p* or its negation. In general, a conflict between two candidates for belief is equipollent for the Sceptic if and only if there is some candidate for belief *p* such that it appears to the Sceptic that there is no reason to believe either *p* or its negation. And, according to Sextus, if it appears to the Sceptic that there is no reason to believe either *p* or its negation, he suspends judgement about whether *p*.

It is a striking fact that Sextus often describes the Sceptic's suspension of judgement as a matter of *necessity*. If it appears to the Sceptic that there is no reason to believe either *p* or its negation, Sextus often writes not that the Sceptic *does* or *will* suspend judgement about whether *p*, but that it is *necessary*, or that the Sceptic is *compelled*, to do so.[8] But what kind of necessity does Sextus have in view when he describes the Sceptic's suspension of judgement in this way?

There appears to be a straightforward answer to this question: the necessity Sextus attributes to the Sceptic's suspension of judgement is *causal* necessity. According to Sextus it is not the case merely that there is a constant conjunction of one type of psychological state (the appearance that there is no reason to believe either *p* or its negation) with another (suspension of judgement whether about *p*). There is also, Sextus claims, a necessary causal connection between these two types of psychological state: its appearing to the Sceptic that there is no reason to believe either *p* or its negation *prevents* the Sceptic from assenting

---

[7] Though it is rarely formulated explicitly, I take this to be the standard view of equipollence. See e.g. Burnyeat, 'Can the Sceptic Live his Scepticism?', 44. But no standard view goes unchallenged, and for a challenge to this view of equipollence see Williams, 'Scepticism without Theory', 555–6. Williams, however, ignores the role the Agrippan modes play in establishing that a conflict between candidates for belief is equipollent.

[8] In some passages Sextus writes that it is necessary for the Sceptic to suspend judgement (ἀνάγκη or δεῖ ἐπέχειν, *PH* 1.61, 1.140, 1. 163, 1.170, 1.175, 2.192, 3.6, 3.29), and in others he writes that the Sceptic is compelled to suspend judgement (ἐπέχειν ἀναγκάζεται, *PH* 1.78, 1.121, 1.128, 1.129, 2.95, and 3.65).

either to *p* or to its negation and thereby *causes* him to suspend judgement about whether *p*.[9]

Sextus is himself a Sceptic (he uses the first person pronoun throughout the *Outlines of Pyrrhonism*), and as a Sceptic he has at his disposal a battery of arguments against causation. These arguments target the claim that there are causes, and having presented them together with arguments in support of this claim Sextus writes that 'it is necessary to suspend judgement about the existence of causes (ἐπέχειν ἀνάγκη καὶ περὶ τῆς ὑποστάσεως τοῦ αἰτίου)' (*PH* 3.29). But if Sextus as a Sceptic suspends judgement about the existence of causes, then for any two things *A* and *B* he suspends judgement about whether *A* is the cause of *B*. But it is clear from Sextus' text that the Sceptic will make utterances of the form '*A* causes *B*' and that these utterances are to be understood as the Sceptic's report that it appears to him that *A* causes *B* where its so appearing to the Sceptic does not imply that he assents to the appearance or proposition, and so believes, that *A* causes *B*. So, on the present line of thought, in claiming that it is necessary for the Sceptic to suspend judgement, Sextus is reporting at a minimum that it appears to him (or to any Sceptic) that a psychological state of one type (the appearance that there is no reason to believe either *p* or its negation) causes a psychological state of another type (suspension of judgement about whether *p*). But someone who accepts this line of thought might also be inclined to think, in addition, that Sextus is reporting something about the way in which he (or any Sceptic) experiences suspension of judgement. Insofar as Sextus (or any Sceptic) cannot avoid or refrain from suspending judgement about whether *p* if it appears to him that there is no reason to believe either *p* or its negation, Sextus (or any Sceptic) experiences suspension of judgement as something that is forced on him and with respect to which he is passive. It is this experience of passivity, of suspension of judgement as something that

---

[9] I take this view to be implicit in the claim in Barnes, 'Pyrrhonism, Belief, and Causation', 2649, that 'the Pyrrhonist's arguments are causally efficacious: they do not provide reasons which we ought to accept; rather they are thought of as working on us like drugs, causing or inducing ἐποχή.' See also Williams, 'Scepticism without Theory', 572. More generally, I take this view to be the view of those commentators who describe the situation in which it appears to a person that there is no reason to believe either *p* or its negation as one in which 'it is psychologically impossible' for her to believe either *p* or its negation. See Burnyeat, 'Can the Sceptic Live his Scepticism?', 44 (who cites Epictetus' challenge at *Discourses* 1.28.14—just try to believe that the number of stars is or is not even—as a reference to this kind of psychological impossibility); Bailey, *Sextus Empiricus and Pyrrhonean Scepticism*, 121–2; and Striker, 'Historical Reflections on Classical Pyrrhonism and Neo-Pyrrhonism', 16.

simply happens to one, that Sextus is also reporting in claiming that it is necessary to suspend judgement.

The view that the necessity attached to the Sceptic's suspension of judgement is causal cannot, however, be the whole story. In this chapter I argue, first, that according to Sextus the Sceptic, in virtue of being a Sceptic, aims to satisfy a basic rational requirement and the fact that he does so is the source of the necessity attached to his suspension of judgement. In the first instance this necessity is not causal but *hypothetical*: it is necessary for the Sceptic to suspend judgement *if* he is to satisfy, as he aims to do, the demands of reason.[10] The necessity attached to the Sceptic's suspension of judgement is the necessity of a means to an end or goal, namely, the satisfaction of a basic rational requirement.[11] I then argue that the Sceptic has the end or goal of satisfying this and other basic rational requirements because (as I argued in Chapter 1) he is engaged in the search for truth and part of what it is to be so engaged is to have this end or goal.

At *PH* 2.19 Sextus writes, with respect to those dogmatic philosophers who have claimed either that there is or that there is not a criterion of truth (κριτήριον ἀληθείας), that:

They will say, then, that this conflict is either decided or undecided (ἤτοι ἐπικριτήν... ἢ ἀνεπίκριτον). If undecided, they will immediately concede that it is necessary to suspend judgement (αὐτόθεν δώσουσι τὸ δεῖν ἐπέχειν); if decided, let them say by what it will be decided, if we neither possess an agreed criterion nor know whether there is one but are investigating the matter.

There is a similar passage at *PH* 1.175 where Sextus writes with respect to a proposition that serves as the content of a thought that 'If it is said to be subject to an undecided dispute, it will be conceded to us that it is

---

[10] Something like the view I argue for in this chapter is suggested by the remark in Striker, 'Sceptical Strategies', 96, that the Sceptic's argument that a conflict between candidates for belief is equipollent 'leads directly to *epochē*: if we have no reason whatever to prefer any proposition to its contradictory, clearly *the most reasonable thing* is to avoid a decision and keep clear of any positive belief' (my emphasis). If it appears to the Sceptic that suspension of judgement about whether *p* is the most reasonable thing to do, and he suspends judgement about *p because* it appears to him to be the most reasonable thing to do, then he accepts that rationality requires him to suspend judgement about whether *p* if he has no reason to believe either *p* or its negation.

[11] I set aside here the issue, interesting as it is, of whether instrumental necessity—the necessity of a means to an end—is genuine necessity. This is the question of whether, and how, it is possible to parse fully the instrumental relation in non-modal terms. For my purposes it is enough that it is natural and common to describe the instrumental relation in the language of necessity—even if, strictly speaking, doing so misrepresents that relation.

necessary to suspend judgement about it (δοθήσεται ἡμῖν τὸ δεῖν ἐπέχειν περὶ αὐτοῦ).'[12] The person who will make this concession, Sextus makes clear at *PH* 1.173, is the Sceptic's dogmatic interlocutor (ὁ προσδιαλεγόμενος) that is, the dogmatic philosopher. When Sextus says that the dispute about whether *p* is the case is 'undecided' (ἀνεπίκριτος), I take him to mean not only, or not even, that there is an actual disagreement about whether *p* is the case, but that there is no reason to believe either *p* or its negation.[13] Now notice what Sextus does *not* say in these passages. He does not say that if the dogmatic philosopher comes to believe that there is no reason to believe either *p* or its negation, then he *must* suspend judgement about whether *p*—and that this is so in the sense that the dogmatic philosopher's belief that there is no reason to believe either *p* or its negation immediately *causes* him to suspend judgement about whether *p*. Nor does Sextus make the weaker claim that if the dogmatic philosopher comes to believe that there is no reason to believe either *p* or its negation, he *will* suspend judgement about whether *p*. Sextus makes no claim to the effect that the dogmatic philosopher either must or will suspend judgement about a candidate for belief that he, the dogmatic philosopher, believes is subject to an undecided dispute. Sextus says only that if the dogmatic philosopher believes that the dispute over whether *p* is the case is undecided, he will *immediately concede* (αὐτόθεν δώσουσιν) that it is necessary to suspend judgement about whether *p*. But what exactly is Sextus claiming here that the dogmatic philosopher will concede? It seems to me that there are two possibilities. (A) Sextus is claiming that the dogmatic philosopher will concede that there is a necessary causal connection between two types of psychological state: the belief that there is no reason to believe either *p* or its negation and suspension of judgement about whether *p*. (B) Sextus is claiming that if the dogmatic philosopher believes that there is no reason to believe either *p* or its negation, then he will concede that it is necessary to suspend judgement about whether *p in order to do what, at least according to the dogmatic philosopher, it is rational for one to do.* If the dogmatic philosopher believes that there is no reason to believe either *p* or its negation, then he will concede that it is *unreasonable* to believe either *p* or its negation. But if that is so, the

---

[12] I take τὸ νοητόν—which Annas and Barnes, *Outlines*, render 'object of thought', and Mates, *The Skeptic Way*, renders 'thought object'—to be a proposition that specifies an intelligible rather than a perceptible state of affairs, and so a proposition that serves as the content of a thought rather than a perceptual experience.

[13] For this point, see Barnes, *The Toils of Scepticism*, 31–2.

dogmatic philosopher will concede that the *only* reasonable thing to do—and so, as a matter of rationality, what one is *required* to do—is to suspend judgement about whether *p*.

(A) and (B) are each possible readings of the claim Sextus makes at *PH* 2.19 and 1.175, but it seems to me that (B) is more plausible. The dogmatic philosopher from whom Sextus claims to extract a concession is someone who, in forming and maintaining his beliefs, at least attempts to satisfy the requirements of rationality as he understands them. And any dogmatic philosopher with whom the Sceptic engages will accept as a rational requirement

(SJ) Rationality requires one to suspend judgement about whether *p* if one believes there is no reason to believe either *p* or its negation.

(SJ) is derived from a more basic rational requirement

(NB) Rationality requires one not to believe *p*, if one believes there is no reason to believe *p*.

(NB), in turn, is just an instance of the more general rational requirement

(R-) Rationality requires one not to have attitude *A*, if one believes there is no reason to have attitude *A*.[14]

The phrase 'rationality requires' as it occurs in the formulation of (SJ), (NB), and (R-) is simply a domain marker. This phrase indicates that the rule or injunction to do *x* if one does *y* falls within the domain of rationality rather than some other domain. In the same way the phrase 'etiquette requires' in

(E) Etiquette requires one to send a thank-you note if one has received a gift.

indicates that the rule or injunction to send a thank-you note if one has received a gift falls within the domain of etiquette. To say that rationality requires one to do *x* if one does *y* is to say no more or less than that doing or having done *y* one must do *x* *if* one aims to follow or comply with, as one might or might not aim to do, the rules or injunctions of rationality.[15]

---

[14] See the discussion of rational requirements in Kolodny, 'Why be Rational?', 515–21. My (R-) is his (C-), but my argument here relies only on the claim that (R-) is *a* rational requirement from which (SJ) is derived, and not (as Kolodny claims) that it is one of the two basic rational requirements from which *all* other rational requirements are derived.

[15] It is plausible to think that there is a kind of necessity that, though not relevant to my exegetical purposes here, is attached to any genuine rational requirement. If a proposition of the form 'It is rational to do *x* if one does *y*' is true, then it is also necessary in the sense that it is true unconditionally or in all possible circumstances. This is what Fine, 'The Varieties of Necessity', has called 'normative necessity'.

A dogmatic philosopher can accept (SJ) (and, by implication, (NB) and (R-)) without accepting that there are or can be reasons for belief. Nor, in virtue of accepting (SJ), is a dogmatic philosopher committed to accepting any particular view about what kinds of considerations, if any, count as reasons for belief. (SJ) is an extremely weak principle, and its extreme weakness makes possible its universal acceptance among the dogmatic philosophers with whom the Sceptic engages. This is not to say that we cannot conceive of someone who rejects (SJ), weak as it is, and has reason to do so. For it is possible for someone to have, as her sole epistemic priority, the acquisition of some true beliefs. For a person of this sort it will be of no importance, or at any rate of considerably less importance, to avoid the acquisition of false beliefs. But if a person's goal is simply to acquire some true beliefs—if, that is, her epistemic goals do not include the avoidance of false belief—then she has reason to reject (SJ). For it is very likely that anyone who accepts (SJ) and is guided by it in her epistemic conduct will fail to maximize her true beliefs. This is so because it is very likely she will suspend judgement about whether p, and so fail to believe that p, when it is true that p, and so when, had she come to believe that p, she would have acquired a true belief. And this is so, in turn, because it is very likely that on at least some occasions, and for any of a variety of reasons, a person will have no access to those considerations that are evidence of the truth of p. So a person with the limited epistemic goal of acquiring some true beliefs has a reason to reject—that is, not to satisfy—(SJ).

The dogmatic philosopher with whom Sextus engages, however, has (as most of us most of the time do) different, and more demanding, epistemic priorities. No one, the dogmatic philosopher included, aims to believe everything that is true. This is so, in part, because for each person there is an indefinitely large number of propositions or candidates for belief to whose truth value that person is indifferent. The range of propositions or candidates for belief to whose truth value a person is *not* indifferent constitute that person's domain of epistemic concern. Within his domain of epistemic concern the dogmatic philosopher aims not only to maximize his true beliefs but also, and no less, to minimize his false beliefs. But to say this is just to say that for the relevant range of values for p, the dogmatic philosopher aims to believe p if, but only if, p is true. If this is so, the dogmatic philosopher aims, *inter alia*, to satisfy (SJ) in forming, retaining, and revising his beliefs. For anyone with the goal of maximizing his true beliefs and minimizing his false beliefs aims to believe all and only those candidates for belief whose truth he believes the evidence favours. But to have this aim is just to aim to believe *p* if, but only if, one believes that there is a certain kind of reason—namely, evidence of the truth of *p*—to believe *p* rather than its negation. Someone with this aim also aims to believe neither *p* nor its negation if he believes that there is no reason to believe either *p* or its negation. And to have *this* aim is just to have the aim of satisfying (SJ) in one's epistemic conduct—that is, to suspend judgement about whether *p* if one believes there is no reason to believe either *p* or its negation.

If the dogmatic philosopher accepts (SJ), and if he believes that there is no reason to believe either *p* or its negation, then he will concede, and at once, that it is necessary for him to suspend judgement about whether *p if* he is to satisfy, as he aims to do, (SJ).[16] My claim is that, according to Sextus, not only the dogmatic philosopher, but also the Sceptic, accepts and so aims to satisfy (SJ). It is necessary for the Sceptic, as it is for the dogmatic philosopher, to suspend judgement *if* the Sceptic is to satisfy, as he aims to do, (SJ).

Before I discuss the textual evidence in support of my claim, I want to consider two objections that might be raised against it at this point. First, even if the Sceptic accepts and so aims to satisfy (SJ), his acceptance of (SJ) *as formulated* cannot be the source of the necessity which, according to Sextus, is attached to his suspension of judgement. In aiming to satisfy the rational requirements (NB) and (SJ) the dogmatic philosopher is guided by a *belief* about the reasons for a belief. The dogmatic philosopher's *belief* that there is no reason to believe *p*, together with his aim to satisfy (NB), directs him not to believe *p*; and his *belief* that there is no reason to believe either *p* or its negation, together with his aim to satisfy (SJ), directs him to suspend judgement about whether *p*. (NB) and (SJ) require that one not have a belief that conflicts with one's belief about the reasons for that belief. Yet on one plausible interpretation of the scope of Scepticism, the sense in which the Sceptic suspends judgement about *everything* is that he has *no beliefs at all* (or, at least, no beliefs about how things *are* rather than merely *appear* to him to be).[17] But if the Sceptic has no beliefs, then he has no beliefs about the reasons for a given belief: the Sceptic does not believe about any candidate for belief *p* that there is no reason to believe either *p* or its negation. And if this is so, then the Sceptic never satisfies the

---

[16] Cf. Barnes, *The Toils of Scepticism*, 20–1 on *PH* 1.170.
[17] In Chapter 3 I defend a version of this interpretation of the scope of Scepticism.

antecedent of (SJ) and, consequently, is never in a position in which it is necessary for him to suspend judgement in order to satisfy (SJ).

This first objection is sound as far as its goes, but it seems to me not to go very far. According to Sextus the Sceptic's conduct—where conduct is understood broadly to include the formation and revision of attitudes—is guided by appearances. On the interpretation of the scope of Scepticism according to which the Sceptic has no beliefs, the notion of appearance with which Sextus works is *non-doxastic*: in reporting that it appears to him that p the Sceptic is not attributing to himself the belief that p. For an appearance is not a belief, but it is supposed to be a psychological state that can guide conduct in the way that belief does. So in aiming to satisfy the rational requirement (SJ) the Sceptic is guided not by a belief but by an appearance about the reasons for a belief. Its appearing to the Sceptic that there is no reason to believe either p or its negation, together with his aim to satisfy (SJ), directs him to suspend judgement about whether p. For this reason we can formulate the rational requirement the Sceptic aims to satisfy in suspending judgement as

(SJ*) Rationality requires one to suspend judgement about whether p if it appears to one that there is no reason to believe either p or its negation.

where it is assumed that the Sceptic has no beliefs about the reasons to believe either p or its negation.[18] The claim of (SJ*) to be a genuine rational requirement may well seem questionable if the occurence of 'appears' in it is understood non-doxastically. For why should the fact that it merely appears to me that there is no reason to believe either p or its negation have any bearing on whether or not I am being rational in believing p? And, all other things being equal, it should not. But in the Sceptic's case, at least on the interpretation according to which the Sceptic has no beliefs, all other things are *not* equal. For the appearance the Sceptic has about the reasons for believing p controls the attitude (belief, disbelief, suspension of judgement) he takes toward p— just as the belief the dogmatic philosopher has about the reasons for believing p controls the attitude he takes toward p. As a result, its appearing to the Sceptic that there is no reason to believe either p or its negation has the same bearing on whether or not he is being rational

---

[18] Otherwise (SJ*) is false. If it appears to me that there is no reason to believe either p or its negation, but nonetheless I believe that there is a reason to believe p rather than its negation (or vice versa), then it is false that rationality requires me to suspend judgement about whether p.

in believing *p* as the dogmatic philosopher's belief that there is no reason to believe either *p* or its negation has on whether or not he is being rational in believing *p*. At the most general level rationality with respect to belief requires one not to have a belief that conflicts with the attitude that controls the formation, retention, and revision of that belief. Both (SJ) and (SJ*) are instances of this most general rational requirement on belief.

A second objection is that in claiming that it is necessary to suspend judgement Sextus is not making any claim about what it is necessary for *the Sceptic* to do. Instead Sextus is claiming only that given the dogmatic philosopher's commitment to certain rational requirements it is necessary for *the dogmatic philosopher* to suspend judgement.[19] This second objection misses its mark, and to see why it is necessary to distinguish the following two issues. The first issue is whether in claiming that it is necessary to suspend judgement Sextus is making a claim that applies not to the Sceptic but only to the dogmatic philosopher. The fact that Sextus makes the claim that it is necessary to suspend judgement in a context in which, as he explains at *PH* 1.31, he is explaining how *the Sceptic himself* comes to suspend judgement indicates that this claim applies to the Sceptic.[20] The second issue is whether, given that Sextus' claim that it is necessary to suspend judgement applies to the Sceptic, the necessity in question has as its source the Sceptic's aim to satisfy a certain rational requirement. That issue can be settled only by examining closely those passages in which Sextus does claim it is necessary for the Sceptic to suspend judgement.

In several passages Sextus argues, in one way or another, that since it appears to the Sceptic that there is no reason to believe either *p* or its negation, then it is *not possible* for the Sceptic to believe (to assent to) either *p* or its negation, and so it is *necessary* for him to suspend judgement about whether *p*. These passages, however, do *not* settle the question whether the necessity attached to the Sceptic's suspension of judgement is hypothetical or merely causal. At *PH* 1.61, for instance, Sextus writes that 'If, therefore, appearances (φαντασίαι) are different depending on the variations among animals, and it is impossible to

[19] For something like this objection, see Frede, 'The Sceptic's Two Kinds of Assent and the Question of the Possibility of Knowledge', 131–3.

[20] In introducing at *PH* 1.31 his exposition of the Ten Modes for suspending judgement Sextus writes that 'it would be appropriate to say how suspension of judgement comes to be *in us* (ἡμῖν)'. And in the course of that exposition Sextus claims on no less than eight occasions (*PH* 1.61, 1.78, 1.89, 1.121, 1.128, 1.129, 1.140, 1.163) that it is necessary—for the Sceptic—to suspend judgement.

decide among them (ἅς ἐπικρῖναι ἀμήχανόν ἐστιν), then it is necessary to suspend judgement about external existing objects (ἐπέχειν ἀνάγκη περὶ τῶν ἐκτὸς ὑποκειμένων).' Here Sextus writes that

if (A) there is a conflict between candidates for belief
     and
    (B) it is impossible to decide this conflict
then (C) it is necessary to suspend judgement.[21]

Now in claiming in (B) that it is impossible to decide a conflict between candidates for belief, Sextus is claiming that for some value of *p* it is impossible to believe (assent to) either *p* or its negation. Since the necessity of suspending judgement about whether *p* is supposed to be a consequence of the impossibility of believing either *p* or its negation, the kind of possibility with respect to which Sextus in (B) claims that it is impossible to believe either *p* or its negation is the same kind of possibility with respect to which Sextus in (C) claims that it is necessary—that is, not possible not—to suspend judgement about whether *p*. So what kind of possibility does Sextus have in view in (B)? At *PH* 1.60–1 Sextus argues for (B) by arguing that it appears to the Sceptic that there is no reason to believe either *p* or its negation. Yet there are two general ways in which Sextus might think that the fact that it appears to the Sceptic that there is no reason to believe either *p* or its negation renders it impossible for the Sceptic to believe either *p* or its negation. For Sextus might think that its appearing to the Sceptic that there is no reason to believe either *p* or its negation *causes* him to suspend judgement about whether *p*. Alternatively, Sextus might think that it makes it the case that the Sceptic must suspend judgement *if* the Sceptic is to satisfy, as he aims to do, the rational requirement (SJ). In this and other passages in the *Outlines of Pyrrhonism* Sextus presents the fact that it appears to the Sceptic that there is no reason to believe either *p* or its negation as the reason why it is necessary for the Sceptic to suspend judgement about whether *p*. But in doing so Sextus raises rather than answers the question we are asking about the necessity attached to the Sceptic's suspension of judgement.[22]

---

[21] If an appearance (or, more accurately, the proposition that serves as the content of an appearance) is a candidate for belief, then Sextus' claim here that animals of different species have different appearances is equivalent to the claim that there are different candidates for belief about a given matter. Moreover, these candidates for belief are not merely different, but different and conflicting. If this were not the case, then there would be no need to decide among them.

[22] See *PH* 1.78, and cf. 1.121, and 3.29. At *PH* 1.78 Sextus argues that if (*a*) the appearances of (what, according to the dogmatists, are) non-rational animals are no less

Sextus sometimes writes that since (1) it is not possible to *assert* (ἀποφαίνεσθαι, λέγειν) either *p* or its negation, (2) it is necessary to suspend judgement about whether *p* (*PH* 1.123, 1.128, 1.140, 1.170). Sextus argues for (1) by arguing that a certain condition holds and that this condition makes it impossible to assert either *p* or its negation. But if (1) is taken literally, then it is false, and obviously so, that the conditions to which Sextus refers—e.g. that everything is relative (*PH* 1.140), or that there is an undecided dispute over the truth of *p* (*PH* 1.170)—make it impossible to assert either *p* or its negation. Since this is so, (1) is not to be taken literally but is to be understood as the claim that (1*) it is not *rational* to assert either *p* or its negation.[23] But if (1) is understood as (1*), then (2) follows from (1) only if (2), in turn, is understood as the claim that it is necessary to suspend judge-ment *if* one is to do what it is rational to do. Now this reading of these passages is plausible—in fact, I think it is correct—but it is not man-datory, and for this reason these passages do not settle the question about the kind of necessity attached to the Sceptic's suspension of judgement. For in these passages Sextus might be using a strict notion of assertion according to which an assertion is an expression of belief (or of assent to a candidate for belief): I can assert *p* if and only if I believe *p*. If I do not believe *p*, I can utter *p*, but my utterance is not, strictly speaking, an assertion. If Sextus is using this notion of assertion, then (1), the claim that it is not possible to *assert* either *p* or its negation, implies that it is not possible to *believe* either *p* or its negation. (2), the claim that it is necessary to suspend judgement about *p*, would follow

credible (μὴ ἀπιστότερα) than the appearances of rational animals, and (*b*) the appear-ances of non-rational animals conflict with those of rational animals, then (*c*) the Sceptic will be able to say about each existing thing how it appears to him, but on account of the things mentioned (διὰ τὰ προειρημένα) (*d*) he will be forced to suspend judgement about how each thing is by nature. So here Sextus identifies the reason why the Sceptic suspends judgement, though it is not immediately clear from the passage what Sextus takes this reason to be. I understand (*a*) to mean that the fact that it appears to a non-rational animal that *p* is no more or less a reason to believe *p* than the fact that it appears to a rational animal that *p*; (*b*) says that the appearances of non-rational animals conflict with those of rational animals. So if it appears to a rational animal that *p* and to a non-rational animal that not-*p*, and if the fact that it appears to a rational animal that *p* is no more or less a reason to believe *p* than the fact that it appears to a non-rational animal that not-*p* is a reason to believe not-*p*, and if there is no other reason to believe either *p* or not-*p*, then there is no reason to believe either *p* or not-*p*. The fact that it appears to the Sceptic that this is so seems to be what Sextus identifies here at *PH* 1.78, as at *PH* 1.60–1, as the reason why it is necessary to suspend judgement.

[23] See Barnes, *The Toils of Scepticism*, 20–1.

from (1) because it follows from the claim that it is not possible to believe either *p* or its negation. In these passages, as elsewhere, Sextus seems to claim that it is impossible for the Sceptic to believe, and so assert, either *p* or its negation because it appears to the Sceptic that there is no reason to believe either *p* or its negation. Yet, as we have seen, there are two general ways in which Sextus might think that the fact that it appears to the Sceptic that there is no reason to believe either *p* or its negation makes it impossible for him to believe, and so assert, either *p* or its negation. On this reading, then, these passages raise but do not answer the question about the sense in which it is not possible for the Sceptic to believe either *p* or its negation, and so it is necessary for him to suspend judgement about whether *p*.[24]

There are, however, passages in *Outlines of Pyrrhonism* that *do* answer this question. First, there is a passage in which Sextus uses the formula 'it is *right* to suspend judgement' (ἐπέχειν προσήκει) interchangeably with the formula 'it is *necessary* to suspend judgement'. At *PH* 2.96, and just before he rehearses a series of arguments against the existence of signs and proofs in order to counter the arguments the dogmatic philosophers offer for their existence, Sextus writes that by doing so 'we shall indicate briefly that it is right [or one ought] to suspend judgement both about the sign and about proof (διὰ βραχέων ὑπομνήσομεν ὅτι καὶ περὶ τοῦ σημείου καὶ περὶ τῆς ἀποδείξεως ἐπέχειν προσήκει).' At the end of his dicussion of signs, Sextus writes that given the available arguments for and against the existence of signs, 'it is necessary to say "No more do signs exist than signs do not exist" (οὐ μᾶλλον εἶναι σημεῖον ἢ μὴ εἶναι ῥητέον).'[25] According to Sextus, the Sceptic in uttering the sceptical phrase 'no more' (οὐ μᾶλλον) reveals that he is in a condition (πάθος) in

---

[24] Here I should say that it seems to me that Sextus' own use of ἐποχή as the grammatical subject of a range of verbs—περιγίνεται, συνάγεται, εἰσάγεται, ἀκολουθεῖ—does not constitute evidence in support of the causal (or, for that matter, the hypothetical) interpretation of the necessity attached to the Sceptic's suspension of judgement. Sextus describes suspension of judgement as something that comes about in the Sceptic, or as something that is brought about by or follows the Sceptic's arguments, or as a psychological state the Sceptic ends up in. But these descriptions are, as far as I can see, entirely neutral with respect to the question of *how*—that is, whether as a causal necessity or as something required to satisfy a rational requirement—the Sceptic's suspension of judgement comes to be or is brought about by or follows the Sceptic's arguments.

[25] *PH* 2.133. My translation here pays the price of inelegance for accuracy. Annas and Barnes, *Outlines*, offer 'we should no more say there are signs than that there are not', but this rendition suggests that οὐ μᾶλλον ('no more') governs ῥητέον ('it is necessary to say') when, as I try to make clear in my translation, οὐ μᾶλλον is part of what it is necessary to say. Mates, *The Skeptic Way*, gets it right: 'it must be said that it is "no more" the case that signs exist than that they do not.'

which for some candidate for belief *p* he believes (assents to) neither
p nor its negation and so suspends judgement about whether *p* (*PH*
2.190–1). So in claiming that it is necessary for the Sceptic to say 'No
more signs exists than signs do not exist' Sextus is claiming that it is
necessary for the Sceptic to suspend judgement about the existence of
signs. *That* claim is made on the basis of arguments against the existence
of signs introduced by Sextus to counter the dogmatic philosophers'
arguments for the existence of signs, and by doing so to support the
claim that it is *right* to suspend judgement about the existence of signs.
It is clear that here Sextus takes the claim that it is necessary to suspend
judgement to be equivalent to the claim that it is right to do so. Further
evidence of this equivalence is found at the end of Sextus' discussion of
proof where Sextus writes that given the available arguments for and
against the existence of proof, 'it is necessary to suspend judgement
about proof ($\dot{\epsilon}\pi\dot{\epsilon}\chi\epsilon\iota\nu$ $\dot{\alpha}\nu\dot{\alpha}\gamma\kappa\eta$ $\kappa\alpha\dot{\iota}$ $\pi\epsilon\rho\dot{\iota}$ $\tau\hat{\eta}s$ $\dot{\alpha}\pi o\delta\epsilon\dot{\iota}\xi\epsilon\omega s$), as well, saying
"No more proof exists than it does not exist"' (*PH* 2.192). Here again
Sextus says it is necessary to suspend judgement about a matter on the
basis of arguments he introduced in support of the claim that it is right to
do so.

The fact that Sextus treats the claim that it is necessary to suspend
judgement as equivalent to the claim that it is right to do so indicates
that in making the former claim he is not claiming merely that some
prior psychological state causes suspension of judgement. But in what
sense, according to Sextus, is it right to suspend judgement? I can see no
reason to think that Sextus is claiming that it is *morally* right to suspend
judgement—that, like W. K. Clifford, he is claiming that it is wrong in
the sense of immoral to believe something on insufficient evidence.[26] It
is more plausible to think that according to Sextus it is right to suspend
judgement in the sense that it is rational to do so. But the rational
requirements (SJ) or (SJ*) identify what it is rational to do in those
circumstances in which Sextus says that it is right to suspend judgement.
Consequently, the claim that it is right to suspend judgement is equivalent to the claim that it is necessary to suspend judgement *if* one is to
satisfy (SJ) or (SJ*). To say that it is right to suspend judgement in the
sense that it is rational to do so is just to say that it is necessary to suspend
judgement *if* one is to do what it is rational to do.

At *PH* 3.36 Sextus writes, this time in relation to the dispute among
dogmatic philosophers over the identity of the basic material elements

---

[26] Clifford, 'The Ethics of Belief', 186.

(ἀρχαί), that 'If, then, we are unable to assent to all positions about the elements or to any of them, it is right to suspend judgement about them (ἐπέχειν προσήκει περὶ αὐτῶν).' Sextus concludes that the Sceptic is *unable* to believe (assent to) any of the dogmatic philosophical positions on the material elements by arguing that it appears to the Sceptic that he has no reason to do so—where, for now, I am leaving it an open question whether its so appearing to the Sceptic is a matter of his *believing* that he has no reason to assent to any of the dogmatic philosophical positions on the material elements. He argues, first, that the Sceptic is unable to believe *without* proof that e.g. earth and water are the material elements (a view attributed by Sextus to Xenophanes). Sextus does not explain why the Sceptic is unable to believe *p* without a proof of its truth. But if the Sceptic believes *p* rather than its negation, or vice versa, without proof, then he does so in what appears to him to be the absence of any consideration that establishes the truth of *p* over its negation, or vice versa. In that case, however, the Sceptic cannot claim to have settled the dispute over whether *p* is the case, e.g. over whether the basic material elements are earth and water. It still appears to the Sceptic that there is no reason, and so he can offer no reason, to believe either that these are or that these are not the basic material elements. Sextus then argues that the Sceptic is unable to believe *with* proof that earth and water are the basic material elements. This is so because it appears to the Sceptic that any line of reasoning offered as a proof is either circular or regressive. But if it appears to the Sceptic that neither circular nor regressive reasoning constitutes a reason for belief, then if the Sceptic believes *p* with proof it appears to him that he believes *p* without having any reason for doing so. If the distinction between believing *p* with and without proof is exhaustive, as Sextus clearly takes it to be, then it appears to the Sceptic that he has no reason to believe any of the dogmatic philosophical positions on the material elements. Now, and this is the important point, Sextus in this passage moves *from* the claim that it appears to the Sceptic that he has no reason to believe either *p* or its negation *to* the claim that it is right for the Sceptic to suspend judgement about whether *p*. Sextus can do so, however, only by way of a principle that connects its appearing to one that there is no reason to believe either *p* or its negation with the rightness of suspending judgement about whether *p*. (SJ)—or, if the notion of appearance with which Sextus works is non-doxastic, (SJ*)— is a principle of this sort if the claim that it is right to suspend judgement is understood, as I have argued it should be, as the claim that it is rational to do so.

To sum up. The sense in which, according to Sextus, it is necessary for the Sceptic to suspend judgement is not, or not merely, that some prior psychological state causes the Sceptic to suspend judgement. For in at least one passage (*PH* 2.96) Sextus treats the claim that it is necessary to suspend judgement as equivalent to the claim that it is right to suspend judgement. But the latter claim cannot be understood as a claim about a necessary causal connection between suspension of judgement and some prior psychological state. The claim that it is right to suspend judgement is best understood as the claim that it is rational to do so, and so understood it is equivalent to the claim that it is necessary to suspend judgement *if* one is to satisfy, as the Sceptic aims to do, the rational requirement (SJ) or (SJ*). Moreover, in another passage (*PH* 3.36) Sextus implicitly relies on (SJ) or (SJ*) in moving from the claim that it appears to the Sceptic that there is no reason to believe either *p* or its negation to the claim that it is right (in the sense that it is rational) to suspend judgement about whether *p*. So, according to Sextus, the Sceptic no less than the dogmatic philosopher aims to satisfy the requirements of rationality as he understands them. And the Sceptic, no less than the dogmatic philosopher, takes suspension of judgement about whether *p* to be rationally required in the absence of any reason to believe either *p* or its negation. The Sceptic differs from the dogmatic philosopher in the range of values for *p* for which he takes reasons for belief to be absent and so suspension of judgement to be rationally required.

In arguing that the necessity attached to the Sceptic's suspension of judgement is hypothetical in the way I have described, I do *not* mean to deny that this necessity is causal, but only that it is *merely* causal. Two points are worth making in this context. First, I am claiming that, according to Sextus, if the Sceptic suspends judgement, his suspension of judgement appears to him to be necessary for the achievement of an objective he has. The Sceptic's objective is to do what it is rational to do, and in those circumstances in which the Sceptic suspends judgement it appears to him that he *must* do so in order to do what it is rational to do. But an objective, or rather the desire to achieve it, can exert psychological pressure on the person whose objective it is. Suppose that I desire some objective *O*, that doing *x* is necessary for the achievement of *O*, and that I believe that this is so. In doing *x* I recognize that my doing *x* is necessary and that the necessity of my doing *x* is hypothetical—that is, I recognize that I must do *x* if I am to achieve *O*—but it need not be the case that I recognize my doing x as *merely* hypothetical.[27] If my desire for O is sufficiently strong, my doing x is, and is recognized by me to be, something I am caused to do by my desire for O. A hypothetical necessity need not be experienced as merely hypothetical, and I am not claiming that, according to Sextus, the Sceptic experiences the necessity attached to his suspension of judgement as merely hypothetical.

Second, suppose that I explicitly form and revise beliefs with a view to satisfying (SJ). I suspend judgement about whether p if I believe that there is no reason to believe either p or its negation. Each time I suspend judgement I do so in order to satisfy (SJ). But over time, and as a result of explicitly forming and revising beliefs with a view to satisfying (SJ), I develop a disposition to suspend judgement about whether p if I believe there is no reason to believe either p or its negation. This disposition moves me, without any explicit reflection on or appeal to my objective of satisfying (SJ), to suspend judgement about whether p if I believe that there is no reason to believe either p or its negation. Moreover, once I have acquired this disposition, when I suspend judgement it is necessary for me to do so where the necessity is at least in part causal: it is a function of my acquired psychological disposition. I experience my suspension of judgement about whether p as something caused by my belief that there is no reason to believe either p or its negation. Now I do not want to rule out the possibility that, according to Sextus, the Sceptic experiences his suspension of judgement as something caused by a prior psychological state. And that is because I do not want to rule out the possibility that, according to Sextus, the Sceptic acquires a disposition to suspend judgement about whether p if it appears to him that he has no reason to believe either p or its negation. My claim is that even if this is so, the hypothetical necessity I have described is the source of the Sceptic's acquired disposition to suspend judgement and so of whatever causal necessity is attached to the Sceptic's suspension of judgement. The Sceptic is now disposed to suspend judgement under certain conditions because in the past he suspended judgement under those conditions *because it was necessary for him to do so*. Yet the necessity attached to those past suspensions of judgement that produced his current disposition to suspend judgement was hypothetical. In this way a full account of the necessity that is now attached to the Sceptic's suspension of judgement must include an account of the necessity attached to his suspension of judgement in the past, and that necessity was hypothetical.

---

[27] Cf. Williams, *Shame and Necessity*, 76.

There is, in addition to the textual evidence I have cited, another reason to think that, according to Sextus, the Sceptic aims to satisfy (SJ) and the necessity attached to his suspension of judgement is hypothetical and not merely causal. I argued in Chapter 1 that the Sceptic is engaged in the search for truth. I shall now argue that a person cannot be engaged in the search for truth without aiming to satisfy certain basic rational requirements that include (SJ).

The Sceptic, Sextus tells us, does not assent to anything non-evident (ἄδηλον).[28] If a proposition *p* specifies a state of affairs *S* that is non-evident, the Sceptic withholds assent from *p*. Dogmatic philosophers, and the Stoics in particular, draw a distinction between an evident (πρόδηλον, ἐναργές) and a non-evident state of affairs. A state of affairs *S* is evident if and only if it is possible to have direct, non-inferential knowledge of *S*.[29] In Stoic epistemology, at least, the class of evident states of affairs is not restricted to those states of affairs of which it is possible to have direct, non-inferential *perceptual* knowledge. Thus the five indemonstrable argument forms that constitute the basis of Stoic logic are formulated in such a way as to be evident and so neutral with respect to contemporary controversies over the interpretation of logical constants.[30] A state of affairs *S* is non-evident, in contrast, if and only if *S* is known, if *S* is known at all, through an inference from a sign. Thus (to take the ancient examples) I know that there is fire on the other side of the mountain by making an inference from the smoke I observe, I know that the body is ensouled by making an inference from the movements I observe it making, and I know that there are imperceptible pores in the skin by making an inference from the sweat I observe flowing through its surface.[31] Now the Sceptic argues that some or all of those states of affairs the dogmatic philosopher classifies as evident are in fact non-evident. The Sceptic argues that the class of evident states of

---

[28] *PH* 1.13: οὐδενὶ γὰρ τῶν ἀδήλων συγκατατίθεται ὁ Πυρρώνειος. See also *PH* 1.16, 1.197, 1.202, 1.210.
[29] *PH* 2.97–9; *M* 8.141, 8.149, 8.316, 8.364. At *PH* 2.97 Sextus reports that according to the dogmatic philosophers evident states of affairs are 'the things that come to our knowledge of themselves' (τὰ ἐξ ἑαυτῶν εἰς γνῶσιν ἡμῖν ἐρχόμενα); and at *PH* 2.99 evident states of affairs are said 'to be knowable of themselves' (ἐξ ἑαυτῶν ... καταλαμβάνεσθαι).
[30] For the Stoic indemonstrable (ἀναπόδεικτοι) arguments, see D.L. 7.79–81.
[31] *PH* 2.97–101; *M* 8.141, 8.145–7, 8.316–19. I gloss over here the Stoic division of non-evident states of affairs into (*a*) those that are non-evident 'once and for all' (τὰ καθάπαξ ἄδηλα), (*b*) those that are non-evident 'at the moment' (τὰ πρὸς καιρὸν ἄδηλα), and (*c*) those that are non-evident 'by nature' (τὰ φύσει ἄδηλα). Those states of affairs in (*a*) are not knowable at all; and the kind of sign by which states of affairs in (*b*) are known (the 'recollective' (ὑπομνηστικόν) sign) is different from the kind of sign by which states

affairs is either empty or limited to appearances.[32] But the Sceptic need not reject the notion of an evident state of affairs as incoherent or unintelligible, and so he need not reject the distinction between an evident and a non-evident state of affairs. And, in fact, Sextus frequently appeals to this distinction in his outline presentation of the Sceptical way of life.

Suppose that *p* specifies a non-evident state of affairs *S*. If I assent to *p*, it does not follow that the belief I acquire by doing so is false or defective in any way at all. However, given the dogmatic philosophical distinction between an evident and a non-evident state of affairs, it is possible for a belief acquired by assenting to a proposition that specifies a non-evident state of affairs to be defective in a way that *no* belief acquired by assenting to a proposition that specifies an evident state of affairs can be. If *p* specifies a non-evident state of affairs, it is possible for my belief that *p*, even if true, to be *unjustified*. Different dogmatic theories of knowledge identify different conditions a belief about a non-evident state of affairs must satisfy in order to be justified. According to the Stoics, for instance, if *p* specifies a state of affairs of kind *S* that is non-evident to me now but it has been evident to me in the past, then my belief that *p* is justified if and only if a second state of affairs of kind *S** is evident to me now and the conjunction of states of affairs of kinds *S* and *S** has been evident to me in the past.[33] However, if *S* is a state of affairs that is 'non-evident by nature' (φύσει ἄδηλον), then my belief that *p* is justified if and only if a second state of affairs *S** is evident to me and stands to *S* as the antecedent stands to the consequent in a sound conditional.[34] The important point here is that *any* dogmatic theory of knowledge identifies a condition—call it a justification condition— that a belief about a non-evident state of affairs must satisfy in order to

of affairs in (*c*) are known (the 'indicative' (ἐνδεικτικόν) sign). At *PH* 2.102 Sextus explains that the Sceptic himself makes use of recollective signs and argues against, and suspends judgement about, the existence of indicative signs. So when Sextus claims that the Sceptic does not assent to anything non-evident, he may mean more specifically that the Sceptic does not assent to any proposition that specifies a state of affairs that is non-evident 'by nature'. Cf. Bailey, *Sextus Empiricus and Pyrrhonean Scepticism*, 125–6.

[32] I think that Jacques Brunschwig, 'Sextus Empiricus and the *kritērion*: The Skeptic as Conceptual Legatee', 240 is mistaken in claiming that for the Sceptic the class of evident states of affairs must be empty. The Sceptic need only argue that for any non-evident state of affairs *S*, there is no evident state of affairs *S** related to *S* in such a way that it is possible to make a valid inference from *S** to *S*.

[33] See *PH* 2.100 and *M* 8.152–3 for the Stoic account of 'recollective' (ὑπομνηστικά) signs.

[34] See *PH* 2.101, 2.104, and *M* 8.245 for the Stoic definition of an 'indicative' (ἐνδεικτικόν) sign.

be justified. This is a condition whose satisfaction is supposed to be conducive to the formation of true beliefs about non-evident states of affairs. A dogmatic theory of knowledge can concede that it is possible for a belief that fails to satisfy the justification condition to be true. It can also concede that it is possible for a belief that satisfies the justification condition to be false. It is possible for an unjustified belief to be true and for a justified belief to be false. But a dogmatic theory of knowledge maintains that even though this is so, a person who consistently forms beliefs about non-evident states of affairs that fail to satisfy its justification condition will, at least in the long run, have fewer true beliefs and more false beliefs about non-evident states of affairs. A dogmatic theory of knowledge identifies a condition as a *justification* condition on a belief about a non-evident state of affairs precisely because it takes the satisfaction of this condition by a belief of this kind to make probable the truth of that belief.

If *p* specifies a non-evident state of affairs *S*, then there are in general two ways in which I can form the belief that *p*. For my belief that *p* either is or is not the product of an inference from some state of affairs that is evident to me and that I take to be evidence of the truth of *p*, i.e. evidence that *S* obtains. I argued in Chapter 1 that, according to Sextus, the Sceptic, in virtue of being a Sceptic rather than a dogmatic philosopher, is engaged in the search for truth. As someone who is engaged in the search for truth, the Sceptic aims to form any belief he does form in such a way that it appears to him that any belief formed in this way is, or at least is likely to be, true. Certain complications aside, the Sceptic—or anyone engaged in the search for truth—aims to form any belief he does form in a way that appears to him to yield true and only, or at least mostly, true beliefs.[35] Now suppose the Sceptic forms the belief that *p* and his belief that *p* is *not* the product of an inference from some state of affairs that is evident to him and that he takes to be evidence of the truth of *p*. Suppose, that is, that the Sceptic forms his belief that *p* without

---

[35] As Williams, *Descartes: The Project of Pure Inquiry*, 42–6 notes, Gettier cases are cases in which a person acquires a true belief by using a reliable method (e.g. common social observation together with valid inference), but the features of that method in virtue of which it is reliable make no contribution to that person's acquisition of her true belief. In these cases the truth of the belief acquired is accidental relative to the method by which the belief was acquired. So merely using a reliable method for acquiring true beliefs does not by itself guarantee that the truth of any true belief so acquired is not accidental relative to the method. Consequently, anyone engaged in the search for truth aims not only to use a reliable method in forming any belief she does form, but also to be led to form any belief she does form by those features of the method she uses in virtue of which it is a reliable method.

making any inference at all or by making an inference from something that he does not take to be evidence of the truth of p. The Sceptic's belief that p might be true: it is possible for a belief about a non-evident state of affairs formed in this way to be true. But even if his belief that p is true, it will appear to the Sceptic that the way in which he formed his belief that p is *not* a way of forming beliefs that yields true and only, or at least mostly, true beliefs. It will appear to the Sceptic that if his belief that p is true, its truth is accidental relative to the way in which he formed it. That is why the Sceptic, or anyone engaged in the search for truth, aims to form any belief he does form about a non-evident state of affairs by making an inference from a state of affairs that is evident to him and that he takes to be evidence of the truth of the belief he forms. This is the only way of forming beliefs about non-evident states of affairs that will appear to the Sceptic, or anyone engaged in the search for truth, to yield true and only, or at least mostly, true beliefs.

The upshot of this line of thought is that aiming to form one's beliefs in a certain way is constitutive of being engaged, as Sextus says the Sceptic is, in the search for truth. A person simply doesn't count as aiming to discover the truth unless she aims to form her beliefs in a way that she believes yields true and only, or mostly, true beliefs. So for any proposition p that specifies a non-evident state of affairs, the Sceptic aims to believe p if, but only if, it appears to him that there is some state of affairs that is both evident to him and evidence of the truth of p— where, once again, I am leaving it an open question, for now, whether its so appearing to the Sceptic is a matter of his *believing* there is a reason to believe p rather than its negation. If this is so, then the Sceptic aims to believe p if, but only if, it appears to him that there is a certain kind of reason—namely, evidence of the truth of p—to believe p rather than its negation. Yet insofar as the Sceptic aims to believe p if, but only if, a certain condition is satisfied, he *also* aims *not* to form the belief that p if this condition is *not* satisfied. That is, the Sceptic aims not to believe p if it does not appear to him that there is a reason, in the form of evidence of the truth of p, to believe p.[36] So the Sceptic aims, *inter alia*, not to believe p if it appears to him that there is no reason to believe p. But to have this aim is just to have the aim of satisfying the rational

---

[36] There are, of course, other ways in which it can fail to appear to the Sceptic that there is a reason to believe p, e.g. if the Sceptic suspends judgement about the matter. The point relevant to my purposes is that if the Sceptic aims to believe p only if it appears to him that there is a reason to believe p, then he aims not to believe p if it fails to appear to him that there is a reason to believe p in *any* of the ways in which it can fail to appear to him that there is a reason to believe p. And one of those ways is if it appears to the Sceptic that there is no reason to believe p.

requirement (NB). (Recall that (NB) states that rationality requires one not to believe *p*, if one believes there is no reason to believe *p*.) If the Sceptic has *this* aim, it follows that he *also* aims not to believe either *p* or its negation—that is, he aims to suspend judgement about whether *p*— if it appears to him that there is no reason to believe either *p* or its negation. And to have *this* aim is just to have the aim of satisfying the rational requirement (SJ).[37] Any dogmatic philosopher who is engaged in the search for truth will also aim to satisfy (SJ). He will have this aim not because he is a dogmatic philosopher and accepts a particular dogmatic theory of knowledge, but because having this aim is part of what it is to be engaged in the search for truth, that is, to have the more general aim of discovering the truth.[38] Since Sextus claims that the Sceptic is engaged in the search for truth, he claims by implication that the Sceptic aims to satisfy (SJ). Thus if it appears to the Sceptic that there is no reason to believe either *p* or its negation, then it is necessary for him to suspend judgement about whether *p* if the Sceptic is to satisfy, as he aims to do, (SJ).

There is, needless to say, no text in which Sextus himself attributes the aim of satisfying (SJ) to the Sceptic. But my claim is that the Sceptic has this aim in virtue of being, as Sextus says he is, engaged in the search for truth.[39]

Sextus distinguishes the stance the Sceptic takes toward suspension of judgement from the stance that, according to Sextus, the Academic Arcesilaus took toward it. It is important that he do so because, at least as Sextus understands the matter, Arcesilaus is similar to the Sceptic in other very important respects. For Sextus writes that Arcesilaus' way of life (ἀγωγή) and the Sceptic's are 'nearly the same' (μίαν σχεδόν), and this is so because Arcesilaus, like the Sceptic, refrains from making assertions about what is the case and suspends judgement about everything (*PH* 1.232). According to Sextus, however,

---

[37] Again, as I noted earlier, if the interpretation of the scope of Scepticism according to which the Sceptic has *no* beliefs is correct, then (SJ) can be formulated as (SJ*). (NB), in turn, can be formulated as: (NB*) rationality requires one not to believe *p* if it appears to one that there is no reason to believe *p*.

[38] This is why having the satisfaction of (SJ) as an aim does not by itself constitute a dogmatic theoretical basis for Scepticism of the sort Williams, 'Scepticism without Theory', has rightly criticized some commentators for attributing to Sextus.

[39] To this extent the Sceptic as Sextus describes him is committed to (SJ). This commitment is more than merely a matter of, as Richard Bett has recently expressed it, *proceeding in accordance with* (SJ) or other requirements of rationality (see Bett, 'What Kind of Self Can a Greek Sceptic Have?', 146 and n. 10). The Sceptic's commitment to (SJ), and to other requirements of rationality, is at least as robust as his commitment to the search for truth—for, I have argued, having the former commitment is part of what it is to have the latter commitment.

He [Arcesilaus] also says that particular suspensions of judgement are good and particular assents bad. Yet someone might say that we say these things in accordance with what is apparent to us, not dogmatically, whereas he says them with reference to the nature of things (ἡμεῖς μὲν κατὰ τὸ φαινόμενον ἡμῖν ταῦτα λέγομεν καὶ οὐ διαβεβαιωτικῶς, ἐκεῖνος δὲ ὡς πρὸς τὴν φύσιν)—so he says that suspension of judgement is a good thing and assent a bad thing (ὥστε καὶ ἀγαθὸν μὲν εἶναι αὐτὸν λέγειν τὴν ἐποχήν, κακὸν δὲ τὴν συγκατάθεσιν). (*PH* 1.232–3)

Sextus attributes to Arcesilaus the claim that in certain circumstances suspension of judgement is good and assent, or the formation of a belief, is bad. So, according to Sextus, Arcesilaus characterized suspension of judgement as something that in certain circumstances a person *ought* to do because in those circumstances it is what it is good for that person to do. It is not clear from Sextus' remarks *why* Arcesilaus claimed that suspension of judgement is good, but one obvious possibility is that Arcesilaus thought that in certain circumstances it is *rational* for a person to suspend judgement *and* that it is good for a person to do what it is rational for him to do.[40] It might appear, in any case, that the distinction Sextus draws between Arcesilaus' and the Sceptic's stance toward suspension of judgement is the following. Even if, like the Sceptic, Arcesilaus regards suspension of judgement as something in certain circumstances it is rational for a person to do, he also, unlike the Sceptic, regards it as something that is good.[41] So the difference Sextus identifies between Arcesilaus and the Sceptic is that Arcesilaus, but not the Sceptic, assigns value to those things he takes reason to require.

But this, I think, is not quite right. In Chapter 1 I argued that the Sceptic values the discovery of truth, and that he values it not only as a

---

[40] And Arcesilaus may have thought that this is so because he thought that a person is to be identified above all with her faculty of reason. For an interpretation along these lines, see Cooper, 'Arcesilaus: Socratic and Skeptic', 96–101. According to Cooper, Arcesilaus, following Socrates, 'accepts that reason should be our guide in life, and its perfection in knowledge our goal,' and when Arcesilaus suspends judgement 'he thinks of himself simply as following reason where it leads. *It* leads to suspension, so *he* suspends—because reason says one *ought* to—and that is why he encourages others to do the same' (96). Cooper claims (101–2) that Arcesilaus differs from Sextus' Sceptic in just this respect: the former, but not the latter, accepts reason as a guide to life. But this claim is false if the necessity attached to the Sceptic's suspension of judgement is hypothetical in the way that I have described.

[41] According to Sextus Arcesilaus, or the non-Sceptic more generally, regards some things as good (or bad) where that is a matter of regarding those things as good (or bad) *by nature* (φύσει) or *with reference to the nature of things* (πρὸς τὴν φύσιν). To say that something is good (or bad) by nature, in turn, is (as Sextus indicates at e.g. *PH* 3.179, 3.182, and 3.190) to say that it is good (or bad) for everyone, that is, that it benefits (or harms) anyone in any circumstances. This is an instance of what Bett, *Against the Ethicists*, xiv–xv, calls 'the Universality Requirement'.

means to something else he values, tranquillity, but also as an end in itself. The Sceptic values the discovery of truth insofar as it appears to him that the discovery of truth is something good—where I am still, though not for much longer, leaving it an open question whether its so appearing to the Sceptic is a matter of his *believing* that the discovery of truth is something good. Now insofar as it appears to the Sceptic that the discovery of truth is good, it appears to him that true, but not false, beliefs are good. The discovery of truth is, after all, at a minimum a matter of acquiring true rather than false beliefs. But if it appears to the Sceptic that true, but not false, beliefs are good, then it will also appear to him that forming his beliefs in a way that yields true and only, or mostly, true beliefs is good. If this is so, in turn, it will appear to the Sceptic that *not* forming a belief is in certain circumstances—namely, in the absence of evidence of its truth—good. And, finally, if this is so, then it will appear to the Sceptic that suspending judgement is in certain circumstances—namely, in the absence of evidence of the truth of either a candidate for belief or its negation—good. So whenever it appears to the Sceptic that it is necessary for him to suspend judgement, it will also appear to him that in this case suspension of judgement is good.

If this is right, then the difference between Arcesilaus and the Sceptic is that to the latter, but not to the former, it merely *appears* that those things he takes reason to require are good. According to Sextus, Arcesilaus, unlike the Sceptic, has the *dogmatic belief* that suspension of judgement, as something required by reason, is good. In certain circumstances the Sceptic does say that suspension of judgement is good and assent, or the formation of a belief, is bad, but Sextus explains at *PH* 1.233 that in doing so the Sceptic, unlike Arcesilaus, is simply reporting how things appear to him.[42] Thus Sextus distinguishes the stance the Sceptic takes toward suspension of judgement from the stance Arcesilaus takes toward it by appeal to a distinction he relies on throughout the *Outlines of Pyrrhonism*, namely, the distinction between appearance and dogmatic belief. That distinction, and its implications for the scope of the Sceptic's scepticism, is the subject of the next chapter.

---

[42] At *PH* 1.233 Sextus writes that when the Sceptic says that suspension of judgement is good he is *not* speaking διαβεβαιωτικῶς. Here, as at *PH* 1.4 and elsewhere, Sextus contrasts speaking διαβεβαιωτικῶς (or τὸ διαβεβαιοῦσθαι) with reporting how things appear to one.

3

The Scope of Scepticism

The Sceptic, according to Sextus Empiricus, suspends judgement about *everything*.[1] If the Sceptic suspends judgement about a candidate for belief *p*, he withholds his assent both from *p* and from its negation.[2] The scope of Scepticism is the range of candidates for belief about which the Sceptic, in virtue of being a Sceptic, suspends judgement. Yet despite describing the Sceptic as someone who suspends judgement about everything, Sextus places a restriction on the Sceptic's suspension of judgement and, by doing so, on the scope of Scepticism.

When we say that the Sceptic does not have beliefs (μὴ δογματίζειν τὸν σκεπτικόν) we are not using 'belief' (τοῦ δόγματος) in the more general sense (κοινότερον) in which some say that belief is acquiescing in something (τὸ εὐδοκεῖν τινι πράγματι). For the Sceptic assents to the conditions forced on her in accordance with an appearance (τοῖς κατὰ φαντασίαν κατηναγκασμένοις πάθεσι συγκατατίθεται). For example, the Sceptic when warmed or cooled (θερμαινόμενος ἢ ψυχόμενος) would not say 'I think I am not warm (or cool)'. Rather, we say that the Sceptic does not have beliefs in the sense in which some say that belief is assent to some non-evident matter investigated by the sciences (τὴν τινι πράγματι τῶν κατὰ τὰς ἐπιστήμας ζητουμένων ἀδήλων συγκατάθεσιν). For the Sceptic does not assent to anything non-evident (οὐδενὶ γὰρ τῶν ἀδήλων συγκατατίθεται ὁ Πυρρώνειος). (*PH* 1.13)

Sextus tells us here that there are some things to which the Sceptic assents. If that is so, then there are some things about which the Sceptic does *not* suspend judgement. Moreover, Sextus indicates here that by assenting to

---

[1] See especially *PH* 1.31 for the Pyrrhonist's claim that 'tranquillity follows suspension of judgement about everything' (τὴν ἀταραξίαν ἀκολουθεῖν... τῇ <u>περὶ πάντων</u> <u>ἐποχῇ</u>), and cf. *PH* 1.205.

[2] See *PH* 1.10 where Sextus defines suspension of judgement (ἐποχή) as 'a state of the intellect on account of which we neither reject nor posit anything' (στάσις διανοίας δι' ἣν οὔτε αἴρομέν τι οὔτε τίθεμεν). In its transitive use ἐπέχειν ('to suspend judgement') simply means 'to hold back' or 'to keep in check'. So to suspend judgement about *p* is to hold back assent from both *p* and its negation.

certain things the Sceptic thereby acquires beliefs. For Sextus first identifies a sense of 'belief' (δόγμα) in which the Sceptic does *not* deny that he has beliefs. Sextus then explains why the Sceptic does not deny having beliefs in this sense by saying that there are things to which the Sceptic assents.[3] But the fact that there are things to which the Sceptic assents explains why he does not deny having beliefs in one sense of 'belief' only if the Sceptic acquires beliefs in this sense by assenting to these things.[4] So it is clear from this passage, even if little else is, that according to Sextus the Sceptic has some beliefs, and that the Sceptic's suspension of judgement, and so the scope of Scepticism, is restricted insofar as the Sceptic has these beliefs.[5] As a result an adequate interpretation of the scope of Scepticism must draw a distinction between two kinds of belief such that the Sceptic's having beliefs of the first but not of the second kind is compatible with Scepticism.

Call beliefs of the kind the Sceptic, in virtue of being a Sceptic, lacks *dogmatic beliefs*, and beliefs of the kind Scepticism permits the Sceptic to have *non-dogmatic beliefs*. There are, in general, two ways to draw the distinction between dogmatic and non-dogmatic belief. The first way of doing so is as the distinction between belief about how things *are* and

---

[3] Sextus' use of the particle γάρ to introduce the claim that there are things (namely, his πάθη) to which the Sceptic assents indicates that he is offering this claim as an explanation for the fact that the Sceptic does not deny having beliefs in one sense of 'belief'. Cf. Fine, 'Sceptical *Dogmata*', 94.

[4] For this reason I think the text of *PH* 1.13 does not support Jonathan Barnes's claim, 'The Beliefs of a Pyrrhonist', 74–5, that the Sceptic's acquiescence in something (τὸ εὐδοκεῖν τινι πράγματι) does *not* involve the acquisition of a belief. Cf. Sedley, 'The Motivation of Greek Skepticism', 19–20 and n. 57.

Burnyeat, 'Can the Sceptic Live his Scepticism?', 30–1, argues that according to Sextus when the Sceptic assents to something he does *not* thereby form a belief. For, Burnyeat claims, (1) belief is the accepting of something as true, (2) the Sceptic assents only to statements that report how things *appear* to him, and (3) for Sextus (and indeed for all Greek philosophy) statements of this sort, as opposed to statements about how things *are*, are neither true nor false. The kind of statement to which the Sceptic assents is not the kind of statement that can be accepted as true (or rejected as false), and so the Sceptic in assenting to statements of this kind does not thereby form a belief. For an extended and critical discussion of Burnyeat's view here, see Fine, 'Subjectivity, Ancient and Modern: The Cyrenaics, Sextus, and Descartes', 194–201; and for additional arguments against Burnyeat's claim that for Sextus statements that report how things appear are neither true nor false, see Barnes, 'The Beliefs of a Pyrrhonist', 66 n. 29; Everson, 'The Objective Appearance of Pyrrhonism', 141–5; and Bailey, *Sextus Empiricus and Pyrrhonean Scepticism*, 157–74.

[5] Cf. Frede, 'The Sceptic's Beliefs', 9 who writes with respect to *PH* 1.13 that 'there can be no doubt whatsoever that, according to Sextus, a serious Pyrrhonean sceptic can have beliefs'. But, of course, there can be and is doubt about the *kind* of belief the Sceptic can have.

belief about how things *appear* to one to be. The Sceptic routinely reports how things appear to him to be. In doing so, he relies on a notion of appearance that is *non-doxastic*: it is possible for it to appear to me that *p* without my believing *p*. In reporting that it appears to him that *p* the Sceptic is *not* attributing to himself the belief that *p*—he is reporting that it *merely* appears to him that *p*. On this line of thought the Sceptic reports that it *appears* to him that *p* rather than that he *believes p* to indicate that he does *not* believe *p* but suspends judgement about whether *p*. But the values for *p* here are propositions about how things *are*, e.g. 'The tower is square', 'The honey is sweet', 'Virtue is knowledge', etc. The Sceptic, in virtue of being a Sceptic, withholds his assent from any proposition of this sort and so has no beliefs about how things are. Nonetheless, the Sceptic assents to those propositions that report how things appear to him to be, that is, to propositions of the form 'It appears to me now that *p*'. Consequently, he has beliefs about how things appear to him to be, and having beliefs of this kind is compatible with Scepticism.[6]

The second way of drawing the distinction between dogmatic and non-dogmatic belief is such that the distinction is *not* equivalent to the distinction between beliefs about how things are and beliefs about how things merely appear to one to be. This line of interpretation takes as its starting point the claim that the notion of appearance on which the Sceptic relies is *doxastic*: in reporting that it appears to him that *p*, the Sceptic is attributing to himself the belief that *p*. The beliefs the Sceptic

[6] The interpretation according to which the Sceptic has no beliefs about how things are typically appeals to the claim that the notion of appearance on which the Sceptic relies is non-doxastic. But by itself this claim implies nothing about the scope of Scepticism. For it implies only that in reporting how things appear to him the Sceptic is not attributing to himself a belief about how things are. But, of course, it does not follow that the Sceptic never attributes to himself, or expresses by an utterance he makes, a belief about how things are. That is why, I take it, some commentators claim that, according to Sextus, *any* statement the Sceptic makes is to be understood as a report of how things appear to him to be. So e.g. Burnyeat, 'The Sceptic in his Time and Place', 97, writes that 'Sextus directs us to understand every statement he makes, however expressed, as a record of his experience (*pathos*) telling us how things appear to him (*PH* 1.4, 15, 135, 197, 198–9, 200, *M* XI 18–19).' It is far from clear, however, that Sextus does issue this direction in any of the passages Burnyeat cites. In all of the passages from the *Outlines*—with the exception of *PH* 1.4—Sextus says not that every statement the Sceptic makes, but every statement the Sceptic makes that involves one of the sceptical phrases (σκεπτικαὶ φωναί), is to be understood as a report of how things appear to the Sceptic. The scope of Sextus' claim at *PH* 1.4 is restricted to the matters discussed in the *Outlines*, that is, to the description Sextus provides of Scepticism and its differences from dogmatic philosophy. On *M* 11.18–19, see Bett, *Sextus Empiricus: Against the Ethicists*, 58–9.

attributes to himself in this way are *not* beliefs about how things appear to him to be but beliefs about how things are—that the tower is square, that the honey is sweet, that virtue is knowledge. These beliefs are to be distinguished from those beliefs in virtue of which one is a dogmatist. It is beliefs of the latter kind—dogmatic beliefs—and only beliefs of this kind that the Sceptic, in virtue of being a Sceptic, lacks. This second way of drawing the distinction between dogmatic and non-dogmatic belief obviously invites the question: if a dogmatic belief is *not* a belief about how things *are* rather than merely *appear* to one to be, what exactly is it?

In this chapter I first examine in some detail, and ultimately reject, several answers Michael Frede has given to this question. Frede's views on the scope of Scepticism have been particularly influential and, in my view at least, they have not received the critical scrutiny they deserve.[7] I then turn to the details of *PH* 1.13 and argue that, according to Sextus, the only beliefs the Sceptic has are beliefs about how things appear to him to be. If this is so, then the distinction between dogmatic and non-dogmatic belief is to be drawn in the first of the two ways I have outlined, and the scope of Scepticism is to be defined by the distinction between belief about how things are and belief about how things appear to one to be.[8]

If the distinction between dogmatic and non-dogmatic belief is the distinction between belief about how things are and belief about how things appear to one to be, then a dogmatic belief is identified by its content. Though Frede argues that for Sextus a dogmatic belief is *not* a belief about how things are rather than merely appear to one to be, he, too, *seems* to claim that a dogmatic belief is identified by its content. For Frede writes that the Sceptic 'has no beliefs about how things *really* are' where he glosses these as beliefs about 'the essence of things' or 'the nature of things' or 'true reality'.[9] The Sceptic can believe that

---

[7] A notable exception is Fine, 'Sceptical *Dogmata*', 83–8—a discussion that, unlike mine in this chapter, is devoted principally to the view(s) of belief Frede offers in 'Two Kinds of Assent and the Possibility of Knowledge'. Cf. also Shields, 'Socrates among the Skeptics', 350–3. Versions of Frede's view are endorsed or defended in Brennan, *Ethics and Epistemology in Sextus Empiricus*, 19–52 and Allen, 'The Skepticism of Sextus Empiricus'.

[8] This view of the scope of Scepticism, though a minority one, is not novel. In a series of papers Gail Fine has offered a defence of it that in some respects differs from, but I think complements, the one I offer here. See especially her 'Sceptical *Dogmata*', 'Sextus and External World Scepticism', and 'Subjectivity, Ancient and Modern'.

[9] Frede, 'The Sceptic's Beliefs', 9–10.

(1) The tomato is red

where to believe (1) is, Frede claims, to have a non-dogmatic belief about what the tomato is like and not merely a belief about how the tomato appears to one to be. Yet even if the Sceptic believes (1), he withholds assent from and suspends judgement about whether

(2) The tomato is *really*—in reality or in the nature of things—red

where to believe (2) is to have a dogmatic belief. The distinction between (1) and (2) depends on what Frede calls a 'meaningful contrast between how things are and how things really are,' and understanding the distinction between believing (1) and believing (2) requires understanding 'how it is possible that someone can really believe something to be the case without believing this is how things are in reality'.[10]

Frede argues that the distinction between (1) and (2) is required by the following sort of case.

Suppose, for example, that a particular wine seems quite sweet to me. Someone might explain, it only seems sweet, because I had eaten something sour just before tasting the wine. If I accept this explanation, I shall no longer think that the wine is sweet; at most, I shall think the wine only seems to be sweet. Yet, someone might also try to provide a quite different explanation. He might say that there is, in reality, no such thing as sweetness, no such thing as sweetness in wine; the wine, rather, has certain chemical properties which, in normal circumstances, make it taste such that we call it sweet. It may even be that I am convinced by an explanation of this sort and come to view how things taste in an entirely new light. Nonetheless, such an explanation might seem rather puzzling, because it is not entirely clear how it is supposed to bear on my claim that the wine is quite sweet. Even if I accept this explanation, the wine will still seem sweet, and I shall still think that it is. Thus, in a sense, it will still be true that it does not merely seem as if the wine is sweet, even if I believe that, in reality, there is no such thing as sweetness.[11]

It is not easy to see just how the case Frede describes here is supposed to support a distinction between dogmatic and non-dogmatic belief where that is understood as a distinction between belief about how things are and belief about how things *really* are. And that is, in part, because it is not clear how in this case the claim that 'there is, in reality, no such thing as sweetness' is supposed to be understood. There are, as far as I can see, at least and at most two possibilities. That claim might represent an error theory of our beliefs about the sweetness of things. On a theory of this sort my belief that the wine is sweet is false. If I accept this theory—a known consequence of which is that wine is not sweet—then on pain of inconsistency I cannot also believe that the wine *is* sweet, but at most that the wine merely *appears* to me to be sweet. In believing that the wine merely appears to me to be sweet, I believe that the wine appears to me to have a quality—sweetness—that I believe it does not in fact have. Now I might find that I am unable to give up the belief that the wine is, and does not merely appear to me to be, sweet. If this is so, then I do not, and perhaps cannot, accept an error theory of our beliefs about the sweetness of things. But the case Frede describes is one in which I am 'convinced' that 'there is, in reality, no such thing as sweetness'. And if in being convinced of that claim I accept an error theory of our beliefs about the sweetness of things, then I cannot be said also to believe that the wine *is*, rather than merely *appears* to me to be, sweet.

Moreover, if I believe that the wine merely appears to me to be sweet, then I believe that in tasting the wine I am subject to an illusion. Here, however, it is important to distinguish two kinds of illusion to which I might be subject. In one sort of case—e.g. when I see an oar in the water as bent—the object I perceive has a property of certain type, and for some reason (e.g. defect in my perceptual organs or in the perceptual conditions) I *misidentify* that property with another property *of the same type*. The oar in the water has a shape, and when I see the oar as bent, I misidentify the shape it has. But this is *not* the kind of illusion to which I believe I am subject if I accept an error theory of our beliefs about the sweetness of things and so believe that the wine is not, but merely appears to be, sweet. For I do not believe that I have misidentified a property the wine has with another property of that same type. I believe instead that in tasting the wine as sweet I perceive the wine as having a property of certain type when in fact it has no property *of that type*.

Alternatively, the claim that 'there is, in reality, no such thing as sweetness' might be equivalent to the claim that sweetness is a secondary rather than a primary quality of objects. If it is, then the distinction between beliefs about how things are and beliefs about how things *really* are is to be understood in terms of the distinction between primary and secondary qualities: I believe that x is F if and only if I believe that F-ness is a *secondary* quality of x, and I believe that x is *really* F if and only if I believe that F-ness is a *primary* quality of x. For any x and any F, in suspending judgement about whether x is *really* F the Sceptic suspends judgement about whether F-ness is a primary, and not merely a secondary, quality of *x*. I think it is clear, however, that the sense in which, according to Frede, the Sceptic believes that the wine is, and does not merely appear to him to be, sweet cannot be that the Sceptic believes that sweetness is a secondary rather than a primary quality. Any belief of that sort, and the practice of suspending judgement about what if anything is a primary rather than a secondary quality of objects, requires the Sceptic to accept the dogmatic philosophical distinction between primary and secondary qualities. But there is no evidence in Sextus, and no reason to think, that the Sceptic accepts this distinction and the corresponding identification of 'how things really are' with the primary, but not the secondary, qualities of objects. Moreover, on Frede's view, if the Sceptic did accept a distinction between primary and secondary qualities, he would have to do so without believing about any quality that it is a primary rather than a secondary quality of objects. If the Sceptic believed about some quality, e.g. shape, that it is a primary quality of objects, he would then believe that things are 'really' shaped and so he would no longer suspend judgement universally about 'how things really are'. Yet if the Sceptic does not believe about any quality that it is a primary rather than a secondary quality, it is difficult to see why he would accept the distinction between primary and secondary qualities in the first place.

Sextus himself at *PH* 1.13 at least appears to indicate both that and how a dogmatic belief is to be identified by its content. For Sextus says there that a dogmatic belief is a belief about a non-evident (ἄδηλον) matter investigated by the sciences. So the Sceptic, in virtue of being a Sceptic, suspends judgement about those matters that preoccupy philosophers and scientists, and one might think that it is possible for him to do so while having beliefs about any variety of ordinary matters.[12] Frede claims that at *PH* 1.13 Sextus tells us that

Only those beliefs will count as dogmatic which involve an assumption or claim about one of the nonevident objects of scientific inquiry. Sextus clearly has the theorems of philosophers and scientists in mind, theorems which they attempt to establish in their efforts to go beyond the phenomena and what is evident in order to get a grip on true reality. These are the doctrines which serve to characterize the various dogmatic schools and allow us to distinguish among them.[13]

Frede's remarks here suggest that in his view a belief is dogmatic if and only if its content is a first principle or theorem of a philosophical or

---

[12] Cf. Barnes, 'The Beliefs of a Pyrrhonist', 73–5 on Sextus' use of the term δόγμα.
[13] Frede, 'The Sceptic's Beliefs', 18–19.

scientific theory. But in fact, and surprisingly, his view is that it is *not* the content of a dogmatic belief that makes that belief dogmatic. For Frede writes that if the first principles and theorems of philosophical or scientific theories were the only targets of the Sceptic's suspension of judgement, then

> it would be clear that the sceptic could have all sorts of beliefs about how things are. For our ordinary, everyday beliefs are, in general, not theoretical doctrines, not assumptions that are part of any science. The sceptic would thus be free to have such 'unscientific' beliefs. Actually, however, matters are presumably more complicated. Since the sceptic suspends judgment—either in a restricted or in an unrestricted sense—on every matter, *even those things that are evident to him must, in a certain respect, be nonevident.* Presumably, we need to understand this as follows: everything, if considered only as an object for reason, can be called into question; every question can be regarded as a question to be answered by reason, a question requiring a theoretical answer derived from first principles which are immediately evident to reason. Nothing, looked at in this way, will be evident to the sceptic, not even the most lowly, ordinary belief. *Any belief, whatever its content may be, can be a dogmatic belief; conversely, every belief can be an undogmatic one.*[14]

The distinction between dogmatic and non-dogmatic belief is, Frede claims here, *content neutral.* And that is so because there are different ways in which the truth of any candidate for belief can be, or fail to be, evident. According to Frede there is at least one way in which the truth of *any* candidate for belief is something that fails to be evident to the Sceptic.[15] For any candidate for belief *p*, it is not evident to the Sceptic that there is some philosophical or scientific theory *T* such that the truth of *T*'s first principles is self-evident and *p* can be validly deduced from these first principles. And that, in turn, is because the Sceptic suspends judgement about the truth of any philosophical or scientific theory. But, Frede argues, even if in this way the truth of any candidate for belief fails to be evident to the Sceptic, the truth of at least some candidates for belief might be evident in another way.[16]

If the distinction between dogmatic and non-dogmatic belief is content neutral, then there are only two ways to understand this distinction: either (*a*) as the distinction between two kinds of attitude that can be

---

[14] Frede, 'The Sceptic's Beliefs', 19 (italics added).

[15] Cf. Allen, *Inference from Signs*, 100.

[16] Frede seems to think that if the Sceptic has a perceptual appearance (φαντασία) that, for example, tomatoes are red, then it will be evident to the Sceptic, and he will believe, that tomatoes are red. See 'The Sceptic's Beliefs', 17–18.

taken toward a given proposition, or (*b*) as the distinction between two ways in which a single kind of attitude can be taken toward a proposition. Consider first (*a*). The idea here is that in defining the scope of Scepticism Sextus appeals to a distinction between two kinds of assent and a corresponding distinction between two kinds of attitude that can be taken toward a proposition. The Sceptic gives one kind of assent (non-dogmatic assent) to *p*, and thereby takes one kind of attitude (non-dogmatic belief) toward *p*. But there is a second kind of assent (dogmatic assent) the Sceptic withholds both from *p* and its negation, and by doing so the Sceptic avoids taking a second kind of attitude (dogmatic belief) toward *p*. This line of interpretation obviously invites the question: how is dogmatic belief (or dogmatic assent) different from non-dogmatic belief (or non-dogmatic assent)? The answer Frede, in at least one discussion, has given is that dogmatic belief, unlike non-dogmatic belief, involves *accepting a proposition as true*.[17] The Sceptic, in virtue of being a Sceptic, accepts *no* proposition as true. But this does not prevent the Sceptic from having beliefs of a kind—non-dogmatic beliefs—that do *not* involve accepting a proposition as true.

It is not easy to make sense of a notion of belief according to which believing *p* does *not* involve accepting, to some degree or other, implicitly or explicitly, *p* as true. It is also, admittedly, not easy to argue, without appeal to controversial premises, that this notion of belief is incoherent rather than merely deeply puzzling. But, in any case, there seems to me to be no textual evidence at all in support of the claim that Sextus is relying on this notion of belief in attributing beliefs to the Sceptic.[18] And there is at

---

[17] Frede, 'The Sceptic's Two Kinds of Assent and the Question of the Possibility of Knowledge', 133–8. Cf. also Striker, 'Sceptical Strategies,' 112–14, 'Scepticism as a Kind of Philosophy', 119, and 'Historical Reflections on Classical Pyrrhonism and Neo-Pyrrhonism', 17–18; and for a critical discussion see especially Fine, 'Sceptical *Dogmata*', 83–8. I am not sure how Frede thinks his view in this paper is related to his view in 'The Sceptic's Beliefs'. In both papers, I think, his view is that the distinction between dogmatic and non-dogmatic belief is content neutral, but in 'The Sceptic's Two Kinds of Assent' he seems to understand this distinction as a distinction between two kinds of attitude that can be taken toward a proposition, while in 'The Sceptic's Beliefs' he seems to understand it as a distinction between two different ways in which a single kind of attitude can be taken toward a proposition.

[18] And the only evidence Frede, 'The Sceptic's Two Kinds of Assent and the Question of the Possibility of Knowledge', 134, provides is Sextus' use of the verb εὐδοκεῖν at *PH* 1.13. Frede writes that 'the ordinary use of this verb' can, but (given that it is a synonym for συγκατατίθεσθαι) need not, 'refer to a passive acquiescence or acceptance of something'. But even if this is so, it is far from obvious, and Frede does not explain why, if my acceptance of a proposition is passive, I do not accept that proposition as true. It is also worth noting that when Frede himself in 'The Sceptic's Beliefs', 17–18, discusses Sextus' use of εὐδοκεῖν, he does *not* claim that εὐδοκεῖν denotes a kind of belief that does not involve acceptance of a proposition as true. Cf. Fine, 'Sceptical *Dogmata*', 93.

least one passage in the *Outlines* that is difficult to reconcile with the claim that beliefs of the kind the Sceptic has do not involve accepting anything as true. For according to Sextus in this passage, the Sceptic claims to have *knowledge* of how things appear to him. At *PH* 1.215 Sextus writes that 'Some say that the Cyrenaic way of life is the same as Scepticism, since it *too* says that we apprehend only πάθη (ἐπειδὴ κἀκείνη τὰ πάθη μόνα φησὶ καταλαμβάνεσθαι).' Sextus here reports that someone else has identified Cyrenaicism with Scepticism and that they have done so on the grounds that both the Cyrenaic and the Sceptic claim that we have knowledge only of our own πάθη. Sextus rejects the identification of Cyrenaicism with Scepticism, but he does *not* do so by rejecting the claim that the Sceptic, like the Cyrenaic, claims that we have knowledge only of our own πάθη.[19] He instead explains that Scepticism differs from Cyrenaicism in *other* respects. For the Cyrenaic, but not for the Sceptic, pleasure is the end or goal (τέλος) of life; and the Cyrenaic, but not the Sceptic, asserts that 'external existing things... have an unknowable nature'.[20] Now in claiming to have knowledge of their own πάθη the Cyrenaics are claiming to know how they are affected or acted upon at a given moment in time— for example, as Sextus reports elsewhere, 'that we are whitened or sweetened' (ὅτι... λευκαινόμεθα... καὶ γλυξαζόμεθα).[21] According to Sextus

---

[19] Cf. Fine, 'Sextus and External World Scepticism', 379–80, who notices that Sextus at *PH* 1.215 does *not* say that the Sceptic, unlike the Cyrenaic, disclaims knowledge of his own πάθη and remarks that 'It is tempting to think he does not do so because he *agrees* with the Cyrenaics that only affections [= πάθη] are known.' I succumb here to the temptation Fine describes.

[20] οἱ δὲ Κυρηναϊκοὶ ἀποφαίνονται φύσιν αὐτὰ [τὰ ἐκτὸς ὑποκείμενα] ἔχειν ἀκατάληπτον. Burnyeat, 'Idealism and Greek Philosophy: What Descartes Saw and Berkeley Missed', 27 n. 28 claims that at *PH* 1.215 Sextus merely *appears* to say that the Sceptic claims to have knowledge of his own πάθη because in the passage 'Sextus is in fact reporting, and resisting, someone else's attempt to assimilate Pyrrhonism to Cyrenaic skepticism'. But it does not follow from the fact that Sextus rejects the identification of Scepticism with Cyrenaicism that he also rejects the claim on the basis of which this identification was made—viz. that both the Sceptic and the Cyrenaic claim that we have knowledge only of our own πάθη. And, in fact, Sextus in *PH* 1.215 does not reject this claim. See also D.L. 9.103 where the Sceptics are said to claim that 'we know only πάθη' (μόνα δὲ τὰ πάθη γινώσκομεν). On this passage and its similarity to *PH* 1.215, see Fine, 'Sceptical *Dogmata*', 98 n. 57, and cf. Fine, 'Subjectivity, Ancient and Modern', 207–8.

[21] See *M* 7.191–4 where, at *M* 7.191, Sextus reports that the Cyrenaics 'say it is possible to say infallibly (ἀδιαψεύστως) and irrefutably (ἀνεξελέγκτως) that we are whitened and we are sweetened but it isn't possible to say that that which produces the πάθος (τὸ ἐμποιητικὸν τοῦ πάθους) is white or sweet'. On the Cyrenaic view that we have knowledge only of our own πάθη, see Tsouna, *The Epistemology of the Cyrenaic School*, 31–61; Brunschwig, 'Cyrenaic Epistemology', 252–9; and Fine, 'Subjectivity, Ancient and Modern', 201–6.

the Sceptic, like the Cyrenaic, claims to know how objects in the world affect him without claiming to know what those objects are like in themselves (though the Sceptic, unlike the Cyrenaic, does not deny that we can know what objects are like in themselves). So, for example, the Sceptic will claim to know that honey sweetens or that 'we are sweetened in a perceptual way' (*PH* 1.19) where that is equivalent to knowing that honey appears sweet to him now.²² Now if, as Sextus claims, the Sceptic has knowledge of how things appear to him, and if belief is a constituent of knowledge, then he has beliefs about how things appear to him. But it is difficult to see how it is possible for the Sceptic (or anyone else) to believe *p*, and in doing so *to know p*, without accepting *p* as true. Even if there is a kind of belief that does not involve accepting a proposition as true, it is difficult to see how a belief of this kind could be a constituent of knowledge.

So there is no reason to think, and textual evidence that gives one some reason to doubt, that for Sextus the distinction between dogmatic and non-dogmatic belief is the distinction between belief that does and belief that does not involve accepting a proposition as true. Yet if both dogmatic and non-dogmatic belief involve the acceptance of a proposition as true, it is difficult to see what feature of dogmatic belief can distinguish it *as a different kind of attitude* from non-dogmatic belief. Perhaps, then, if it is a content-neutral distinction, the distinction between dogmatic and non-dogmatic belief is to be understood not as a distinction between two kinds of attitude, but rather as a distinction between two different ways in which a single kind of attitude—the attitude of belief—can be held. Consider, in this connection, the way in which, according to Frede, the truth of *any* candidate for belief is something non-evident to the Sceptic. The Sceptic assents only to those candidates for belief whose truth is evident to him. For Sextus insists that the Sceptic does not assent to any candidate for belief whose truth is something non-evident (ἄδηλον) to him (*PH* 1.13, 1.16). But, according to Frede, even if the truth of *p* is evident to the Sceptic, it is *not* evident to him that there is a sound philosophical or scientific doctrine that establishes the truth of *p*. And that is so because there is no philosophical or scientific doctrine whose truth is evident to the

---

²² It might seem odd for the Sceptic to claim knowledge of how things appear to him, but in doing so he is claiming only that it is evident to him that, for example, honey appears sweet to him now. On the Sceptic's claim to have knowledge of how things appear to him, cf. Everson, 'The Objective Appearance of Pyrrhonism', 137–8.

Sceptic. The Sceptic withholds assent from, and so suspends judgement about the truth of, those claims that constitute a philosophical or scientific doctrine. There is no philosophical or scientific doctrine the Sceptic accepts, and it follows that, though the Sceptic has beliefs, there is nothing the Sceptic believes *on the basis of* a philosophical or scientific doctrine he accepts. This is the respect in which the dogmatic philosopher differs from the Sceptic. The dogmatic philosopher, unlike the Sceptic, has dogmatic beliefs where a belief, regardless of its content, is dogmatic if and only if it is held because its truth is taken to be a consequence of some philosophical or scientific doctrine that is itself taken to be true. On this view, the dogmatic philosopher will have some beliefs the Sceptic lacks—namely, those beliefs that constitute his acceptance of some philosophical or scientific doctrine. But the dogmatic philosopher and the Sceptic will also share many beliefs, and with respect to these beliefs the dogmatic philosopher differs from the Sceptic not in what he believes but in the grounds or basis upon which he believes it.

In fact I think this is the only way to make any sense of a content-neutral distinction between dogmatic and non-dogmatic belief, but so understood the distinction has not exactly left its mark on Sextus' text. According to Frede, Sextus at *PH* 1.20 and elsewhere places an explicit restriction on the Sceptic's suspension of judgement. Sextus explains there that the Sceptic investigates, and so suspends judgement about, whether honey is sweet ὅσον ἐπὶ τῷ λόγῳ where Frede construes this Greek phrase as meaning 'to the extent that this is a question for reason'. Frede's view seems to be that in using the phrase ὅσον ἐπὶ τῷ λόγῳ Sextus is making reference to a special dogmatic notion of reason.[23] Frede writes that for the dogmatic philosopher reason is the faculty 'that can lead us beyond the world of appearances to the world of real beings; and thus for [the dogmatist] it is a matter of reason, what is to count as real and as true, and what is to count as appearance'.[24] The Sceptic suspends judgement about whether reason, as the dogmatic philosopher thinks of it, can establish it as true that honey is sweet. But reason, as the dogmatic philosopher thinks of it, is the faculty by which we identify self-evident philosophical or scientific first principles and make valid

---

[23] But Frede exegesis, as should be abundantly clear by now, is a tricky business, and it is not easy to make sense of his remarks in 'The Sceptic's Beliefs', 9–11.

[24] Ibid. 10.

deductions from them. So suspending judgement about whether reason can establish it as true that honey is sweet is a matter of suspending judgement about whether there are any self-evident philosophical or scientific first principles from which it can be validly deduced that honey is sweet. But suspending judgement about *this* is compatible with believing that honey is, and does not merely appear to be, sweet.[25]

Frede cites Sextus' discussion at *PH* 1.215 of the differences between Scepticism and Cyrenaicism as the principal textual evidence for his claim that the Sceptic's suspension of judgement is restricted to how things are 'insofar as it is a matter of reason'. There Sextus writes that 'we suspend judgement ὅσον ἐπὶ τῷ λόγῳ about external objects (τῶν ἐκτὸς ὑποκειμένων), while the Cyrenaics assert that these objects have an unknowable (ἀκατάληπτον) nature.' Frede claims that the restriction on suspension of judgement expressed by the Greek phrase ὅσον ἐπὶ τῷ λόγῳ 'is not that the sceptic suspends judgment about how things are but not about how they appear; the restriction, rather, is that the sceptic suspends judgment about how things are in a certain respect. That, however, implies that there is another respect in which the sceptic does not suspend judgment about how things are.'[26] But I see no reason at all—and Frede does not give us any reason—to think that Sextus' use here of the phrase ὅσον ἐπὶ τῷ λόγῳ has this implication. For Sextus uses this phrase here to highlight an important feature of the Sceptic's suspension of judgement, namely, that it is a response to a particular argument and that, given what the Sceptic takes to be the force of that argument, it is subject to revision. Someone might suspend judgement about whether some object *x* has some property *F*-ness because she believes, as the Cyrenaic does, that she does not have, because there *cannot be*, any reason to believe that *x* is *F*. But the Sceptic's suspension of judgement is not supposed to be based on any form of negative dogmatism. The Sceptic suspends judgement in response to an argument that purports to show that he does not *now* have any reason to believe about *x* that it is *F* rather than that it is *G*, or vice versa. But the Sceptic, at least, does not take this argument to rule of the possibility of there being a reason, and so of the Sceptic himself coming to have a reason, to believe about *x* that it is *F* rather than that it is *G*, or vice versa.

---

[25] In commenting on *PH* 1.20 Frede, 'The Sceptic's Beliefs', 11 writes: 'We may, thus, assume that the import of this restriction is that the sceptic suspends judgment on how things really are; but that is not the same as claiming that the sceptic suspends judgment on how things are without any restriction.'

[26] Frede, 'The Sceptic's Beliefs', 11.

That is why the Sceptic's suspension of judgement is, and is understood by him to be, subject to revision. So when Sextus writes that the Sceptic suspends judgement ὅσον ἐπὶ τῷ λόγῳ about external objects, he means simply that a particular argument about the lack of a reason to believe one thing rather than another about some external object is the basis upon which the Sceptic suspends judgement. But the claim that the Sceptic has a definite basis for suspending judgement about whether *x* is *F* obviously does *not* imply that there is some respect in which the Sceptic does not suspend judgement about whether *x* is *F*. So *PH* 1.215 provides no support for Frede's claim that Sextus uses the phrase ὅσον ἐπὶ τῷ λόγῳ to refer to a special dogmatic notion of reason and, by doing so, to restrict the Sceptic's suspension of judgement to how things are 'insofar as it is a matter of reason'.[27]

Frede contends that Sextus' discussion of signs (σημεῖα) supports this claim as well (see *PH* 2.97–103, *M* 8.141–299). For Frede claims that, according to Sextus, the Sceptic suspends judgement about the existence of signs in one respect, 'namely, to the extent that one considers this matter for arguments, for reason'—where, again, I take this to mean that the Sceptic suspends judgement about whether there are any self-evident philosophical or scientific first principles from which it can be validly deduced that there are signs. But, Frede continues, though he suspends judgement about this matter, the Sceptic believes that there are signs.[28] Now Sextus' discussion of signs raises a range of difficult issues I cannot address here (and that Frede does not address).[29] But I think at least this much is clear. Sextus presents a dogmatic philosophical distinction between 'indicative' (ἐνδεικτικόν) and 'recollective' (ὑπομνηστικόν)

---

[27] As Brunschwig, 'The ὅσον ἐπὶ τῷ λόγῳ Formula in Sextus Empiricus', 244, notes, the phrase ὅσον ἐπὶ τῷ λόγῳ occurs rarely in Sextus: only four times in *PH* (*PH* 1.20, 1.227 (a passage Frede does not cite), 3.48, and 3.72). Frede also cites, though he does not discuss, a number of passages (*PH* 2.26, 2.104, 3.6, 3.13, 3.29, 3.135) in which what he takes to be a variant of this phrase occurs: ὅσον ἐπὶ τοῖς λεγομένοις ὑπὸ τῶν δογματικῶν. But it is far from clear that in Sextus the phrase ὅσον ἐπὶ τοῖς λεγομένοις ὑπὸ τῶν δογματικῶν is simply equivalent to the phrase ὅσον ἐπὶ τῷ λόγῳ. On this matter see Brunschwig, 'The ὅσον ἐπὶ τῷ λόγῳ Formula in Sextus Empiricus', 246–9. It is, in any case, striking that the phrase ὅσον ἐπὶ τοῖς λεγομένοις ὑπὸ τῶν δογματικῶν occurs only in those sections of *PH* (the second and third books) devoted to the discussion of dogmatic philosophical theories.

[28] Frede, 'The Sceptic's Beliefs', 11: 'Sextus' discussion of signs, thus, is a good example of how, in a certain sense, the sceptic does suspend judgment about how things are—namely, to the extent that one considers this matter for arguments, for reason—but also of how, despite his suspension of judgment, the sceptic does think that, given how things are, there are signs.'

[29] On which see Allen, *Inference from Signs*, 87–146.

signs, and he explains that the Sceptic argues only against the existence of the former kind of sign (*PH* 2.102). So, according to Sextus, though the Sceptic suspends judgement about one kind of sign (the indicative sign), he does not deny the existence of another kind of sign (the recollective sign). There is not, as Frede suggests there is, a single kind of sign such that in one respect the Sceptic believes that there are, while in another respect he suspends judgement about whether there are, signs of this kind. Sextus' discussion of signs offers no evidence that he restricts the Sceptic's suspension of judgement in the way Frede claims.

Moreover, and finally, a text Frede cites but does not discuss is in fact difficult to reconcile with his claim that the Sceptic suspends judgement about how things are 'only insofar as it is a matter of reason'. At *PH* 1.27–8 Sextus rehearses what in Chapter 1 I called *the value argument*.[30] There he argues that anyone who believes that certain things are good and other things bad 'by nature' ($\tau\hat{\eta}$ $\phi\acute{v}\sigma\epsilon\iota$) will be perpetually anxious or distressed. If I believe that x is good, but I fail to possess it, I will believe that my failure to possess x is itself something bad, and so I will be distressed by it. Yet if I possess x, I will fear losing it, and I will be anxious about doing whatever I can to prevent its loss. In either case, then, I experience anxiety or distress: in the first case my distress is the direct result of my belief that the failure to possess x is bad, while in the second case it is the direct result of my fear of losing x, and in both cases it is the indirect result of my believing that x is good. According to the value argument *any* belief about the goodness or badness of something is a source of anxiety or distress. Yet if this is so, then in a range of cases— those that involve questions about the value of something—the Sceptic must abandon the search for truth and pursue suspension of judgement as the necessary means to tranquillity. In Chapter 1 I argued that Sextus has good reason to discard the value argument because it is in tension with his description of the Sceptic as engaged in the search for truth and for Sextus engagement in the search for truth is a central feature of Scepticism as a way of life. However, the value argument is not in tension with anything Sextus says about the separate issue of the scope of Scepticism. For this reason, and despite the fact that Sextus has good reason to reject it, the value argument is evidence of what Sextus takes to be the scope of Scepticism.

[30] This argument differs in certain important respects from the argument for a connection between Scepticism and tranquillity given at *M* 11.111–14. For discussion see Annas, 'Doing without Objective Values', 17–18, and especially Bett, *Sextus Empiricus: Against the Ethicists*.

The value argument does not target any belief that is compatible with Scepticism, that is, it does not target any non-dogmatic belief. If it did, it would have what is for Sextus the unwelcome consequence of showing that some *beliefs* that are compatible with Scepticism are sources of distress or anxiety. Yet if this is so, then Scepticism does not remove, as Sextus claims it does, *all* of those beliefs that are obstacles to tranquillity. The value argument is supposed to show that *only* the dogmatic belief that x is good or bad—a belief the Sceptic, in virtue of being a Sceptic, lacks—is a source of anxiety or distress.

But now the question is why this should be so or why Sextus (or anyone else) would think that this is so *if* the dogmatic belief that x is good differs from the non-dogmatic belief that x is good only with respect to the grounds or basis upon which it is held. Why, that is, would Sextus think that it is the grounds or basis upon which I believe that x is good that determines whether, and to what extent, I am distressed by my failure to possess x or, if I do possess x, anxious about losing it. It is not difficult to see how the belief that something is good or bad can be a source of anxiety or distress. But it is difficult to see how the source of this anxiety or distress can be anything other than the degree to which I believe that something is good or the amount of value I attribute to it. If I strongly believe that something is good, or if I believe that its value or goodness is especially great, then it is plausible enough that I will be distressed by my failure to possess it or, if I do possess it, anxious about the possibility of losing it (provided, of course, that I believe the good in question is the kind of thing which once acquired can be lost). But I can strongly believe that x is good, or believe that the value or goodness of x is especially great, without *also* believing that there is some philosophical or scientific theory from whose self-evident first principles it can be validly deduced that x is good. Yet if we accept Frede's account of the distinction between dogmatic and non-dogmatic belief, then we are forced to read Sextus at *PH* 1.27–8 as claiming that it is the grounds or basis upon which the belief that x is good is held—more specifically, the fact that these grounds are philosophical or scientific rather than ordinary—that is the source of distress and anxiety. And this reading of the argument at *PH* 1.27 deprives it of what plausibility it might otherwise have had.[31]

---

[31] See also Burnyeat, 'Can the Sceptic Live his Scepticism?', 52, who makes a similar point against Frede.

To sum up this part of the discussion. Though Frede in at least one place seems to claim that a dogmatic belief is identified by its content, it is unclear there what Frede takes the distinctive content of a dogmatic belief to be. Moreover, his considered view is that the distinction between dogmatic and non-dogmatic belief is content neutral. But, I have argued, neither of the two (incompatible) accounts Frede has offered of the content neutrality of this distinction is convincing. For there is no evidence in the *Outlines of Pyrrhonism* to support, and at least one passage that raises a doubt about, the claim that dogmatic belief does, and non-dogmatic belief does not, involve the acceptance of a proposition as true. Nor is there any evidence that for Sextus a belief, regardless of its content, is dogmatic if and only if it is held on the basis of some philosophical or scientific doctrine. I conclude, then, that Frede has given us no reason to think that for Sextus the distinction between dogmatic and non-dogmatic belief is *not* the distinction between belief about how things are and belief about how things appear to one to be.

I turn now to the details of the passage, *PH* 1.13, that has been at the centre of the controversy over the scope of Scepticism.

When we say that the Sceptic does not have beliefs (μὴ δογματίζειν τὸν σκεπτικόν) we are not using 'belief' (τοῦ δόγματος) in the more general sense (κοινότερον) in which some say that belief is acquiescing in something (τὸ εὐδοκεῖν τινι πράγματι). For the Sceptic assents to the conditions forced on him in accordance with an appearance (τοῖς γὰρ κατὰ φαντασίαν κατηναγκασμένοις πάθεσι συγκατατίθεται). For example, the Sceptic when warmed or cooled (θερμαινόμενος ἢ ψυχόμενος) would not say 'I think I am not warm (or cool)'. Rather, we say that the Sceptic does not have beliefs in the sense in which some say that belief is assent to some non-evident matter investigated by the sciences (τὴν τινι πράγματι τῶν κατὰ τὰς ἐπιστήμας ζητουμένων ἀδήλων συγκατάθεσιν). For the Sceptic does not assent to anything non-evident (οὐδενὶ γὰρ τῶν ἀδήλων συγκατατίθεται ὁ Πυρρώνειος).

Sextus here as elsewhere identifies a dogmatic belief—the kind of belief the Sceptic, in virtue of being a Sceptic, lacks—as assent to something non-evident (ἄδηλον).[32] The distinction between the evident and the non-evident is a dogmatic one. Sextus reports elsewhere that for the dogmatic philosopher something is evident (πρόδηλον, ἐναργές) if and only if it is known directly or immediately, that is, without inference from something else that is known. Something is non-evident if and

---

[32] *PH* 1.16, 1.198, 1.202, 1.210, 1.219, 1.223. Cf. 1.193, 1.201, 1.208, 2.5.

only if it is *not* known in this way, that is, something non-evident is known, if it is known at all, as the result of an inference from something else that is known.[33] For Sextus a dogmatic belief is a belief about something non-evident and, as such, is the product of an inference.

Sextus also tells us at *PH* 1.13 that there are some things—namely, his own πάθη—to which the Sceptic assents. According to Sextus at *PH* 1.19 when the Sceptic assents to something, and so comes to have a non-dogmatic belief, he does so involuntarily or without willing it (ἀβουλήτως). Now Sextus does not say in either of these passages that the Sceptic assents to something evident. There are, however, at least two reasons for thinking that the object of the Sceptic's assent is something evident. First, this is implied by Sextus' description of the Sceptic's assent as involuntary. For according to the dogmatic philosopher, as Sextus indicates elsewhere, involuntary assent is assent given to something evident.[34] Second, at *PH* 1.13 Sextus claims both that the Sceptic assents to something and that the Sceptic does not assent to anything non-evident. Yet the dogmatic definitions of the evident and the non-evident recorded by Sextus indicate that the distinction between the evident and the non-evident is exhaustive.[35] So if the Sceptic assents to something, but does not assent to anything non-evident, then he assents to something evident. If this is right, for Sextus a non-dogmatic belief is a belief about something evident and, as such, is not the product of an inference.

According to Sextus at *PH* 1.13, then, a dogmatic belief is identified by its content. For it is, as he says there, a belief about something non-evident.

[33] *PH* 2.97, 2.99, *M* 8.141, 8.144. Cf. *M* 7.365–6.

[34] At *M* 8.316 Sextus writes that 'evident are the things grasped *without our willing it* by [or from] an appearance and by [or from] a passive condition (ἐναργῆ μὲν τὰ ἐκ φαντασίας ἀβουλήτως καὶ ἐκ πάθους λαμβανόμενα).' Two points about the grammar of this passage. First, I take ἀβουλήτως to modify λαμβανόμενα: what is said here to occur without our willing it is our grasp of what is evident and not our having the appearance or πάθος on the basis of which we grasp it. Second, I take καί to be epexegetic (as does Fine, 'Sceptical *Dogmata*', 95 n. 49)—to grasp something ἐκ φαντασίας is, given that a φαντασία is a kind of πάθος, to grasp it ἐκ πάθους.

Sextus does not say that a belief about something non-evident, and so a dogmatic belief, is voluntary. But it seems to me that this is the clear implication of both the definition of the evident given at *M* 8.316 and of Sextus' description at *PH* 1.19 of the Sceptic's assent, and so non-dogmatic belief, as involuntary. For Sextus would describe the Sceptic's assent as involuntary only if the Sceptic's assent, and so non-dogmatic belief, differs in just this respect from the assent, and the dogmatic beliefs, of the non-Sceptic. And, though again Sextus is not explicit about this, a belief about something non-evident, and so a dogmatic belief, appears to be voluntary insofar as it is the product of an inference. This is, admittedly, a peculiar conception of doxastic voluntarism.

[35] See especially *M* 8.144 where the evident is defined as what is, and the non-evident as what is not, known of or by itself (ἐξ αὐτοῦ).

Further, a dogmatic belief differs from a non-dogmatic belief not only with respect to its content but also, and for that reason, with respect to the way in which it is acquired. A dogmatic belief is, while a non-dogmatic belief is not, the product of an inference. If this is all that *PH* 1.13 tells us, it does not tell us very much about the scope of Scepticism. For it tells us neither what it is a dogmatic belief is about in being about something non-evident, nor what it is a non-dogmatic belief is about in being about something evident. Before I take up this issue, though, I want to consider two objections to the claim that the scope of Scepticism is to be understood in terms of the dogmatic philosophical distinction between the evident and the non-evident.

The first objection is that there are passages in Sextus where he appears to claim that the Sceptic suspends judgement about things that are evident no less than about things that are non-evident. Yet if this is so, then the Sceptic does not assent to anything evident and a non-dogmatic belief is not to be characterized as a belief about something evident. I think it is clear, however, that this objection misses its mark. According to the dogmatic philosopher we acquire our non-inferential knowledge of evident things through one kind of criterion of truth.[36] The Sceptic, according to Sextus, argues that we ought to suspend judgement about the existence of any criterion of truth of this or any other kind and, consequently, about those matters that the dogmatic philosopher regards as evident. Thus at *PH* 2.95 Sextus writes:

Criteria of truth having appeared perplexing, it is no longer possible to make strong assertions, so far as what is said by the Dogmatists goes, either about what seems to be evident or about what is non-evident. For since the Dogmatists deem that they apprehend the latter from what is evident, how, *if we are compelled to suspend judgement about what they call evident* (ἐὰν ἐπέχειν περὶ τῶν ἐναργῶν καλουμένων ἀναγκαζώμεθα), could we be bold enough to make any assertion about what is non-evident.[37]

---

[36] Brunschwig, 'Sextus Empiricus and the *kritērion*: The Sceptic as Conceptual Legatee', has shown in convincing detail that Sextus' discussions in *PH* 2 and *M* 7 of dogmatic doctrines of the criterion of truth incorporate two distinct conceptions of the criterion: one conception (the Stoic conception of the καταληπτικὴ φαντασία or 'cognitive impression') identifies knowledge through a criterion of truth with non-inferential knowledge; the other conception (according to Brunschwig, the Epicurean conception) identifies knowledge through a criterion with inferential knowledge of non-evident matters.

[37] See also *M* 7.25 and 8.141-2. At *PH* 1.178 Sextus presents the Two Modes that are supposed to show that 'nothing is apprehended either by means of itself or by means of something else'. I take Sextus to be arguing that none of those things the dogmatic philosopher takes to be apprehended by means of itself is in fact apprehended by means of itself. But it doesn't follow that for Sextus or the Sceptic nothing at all is apprehended by means of itself. Cf. Bailey, *Sextus Empiricus and Pyrrhonean Scepticism*, 123-5.

Sextus claims here and in similar passages only that the Sceptic suspends judgement (or ought to suspend judgement) about those matters the dogmatic philosopher regards as evident. But it does not follow from the fact that those matters the dogmatic philosopher regards as evident are not evident to the Sceptic that *nothing* is evident to the Sceptic. And, therefore, it does not follow that there is nothing evident to the Sceptic to which the Sceptic assents and, by doing so, comes to have a non-dogmatic belief. In describing Scepticism Sextus makes use of the dogmatic philosopher's distinction between the evident and the non-evident. But he can do so while disagreeing with the dogmatic philosopher, as he does, about what is non-evident and what, if anything, is evident.

The second objection, raised by Myles Burnyeat, is that the distinction between the evident and the non-evident 'makes no difference to the scope of Sextus' scepticism' because the Sceptic as Sextus describes him does not practise what Burnyeat calls *insulation*.[38] In general a philosopher practises insulation if her ordinary beliefs or attitudes are not regulated—that is, not formed, sustained, or revised—by any conclusion she reaches or any attitude she adopts in philosophical reflection. In the case of modern philosophical scepticism, in particular, a philosopher practises insulation if the doubt a sceptical argument generates does not persist outside the context of philosophical reflection— if, outside that context, the philosopher does not continue to doubt that she has hands or that $2 + 3 = 5$. Philosophical reflection on the arguments of the First Meditation or their contemporary counterparts might lead a philosopher to conclude that a great many of the knowledge claims she ordinarily makes are false. But if she practises insulation, the fact that she has reached this conclusion does not prevent her, outside the context of philosophical reflection, from making these very same knowledge claims in full conviction of their truth. And, finally, the Sceptic as Sextus describes him practises insulation if the fact that in the context of philosophical reflection the Sceptic suspends judgement about whether p does *not* determine the attitude he takes toward p outside of that context. If the Sceptic who practises insulation suspends judgement about whether p outside of the context of philosophical reflection, he does not do so *because* he suspends judgement about whether p within that context.

So, for example, the philosophical arguments for and against the existence of motion appear to the Sceptic to be equally strong. As a result, and in the context of philosophical reflection, the Sceptic sus-

---

[38] Burnyeat, 'The Sceptic in his Place and Time', 115–16.

pends judgement about whether or not motion exists. If he does so, however, then in the context of philosophical reflection the Sceptic also withholds his assent from any candidate for belief—e.g. that the ship in the harbour is moving—whose acceptance he takes to commit one to the belief that motion exists (or, of course, that it does not exist). Now if, as Burnyeat claims, the Sceptic does *not* practise insulation, and if the Sceptic takes a certain attitude toward a candidate for belief in the context of philosophical reflection, then he will *for that reason* take the same attitude toward that candidate for belief outside of that context as well. So the Sceptic who in the context of philosophical reflection suspends judgement about whether or not motion exists or the ship in the harbour is moving suspends judgement about these matters outside of that context, in ordinary life, as well. Moreover, according to Sextus the Sceptic, in the context of philosophical reflection, suspends judgement about whether or not time or place or body exists. Consequently, outside of that context, in ordinary life, the Sceptic suspends judgement about the existence of these things and withholds his assent from any candidate for belief whose acceptance he takes to commit one to the belief that time or place or body exists (or does not exist). That is why, according to Burnyeat, the Sceptic has, or at least claims to have, no beliefs.

Suppose that Burnyeat is right (as, in fact, I think he is) in claiming that the Sceptic does not practise insulation. It does not follow, as Burnyeat seems to claim it does, that the distinction between the evident and the non-evident is irrelevant to the scope of Scepticism. For at most the absence of insulation explains only one aspect of the scope of Scepticism. To see that this is so it is necessary to draw a distinction between (*a*) the range of matters about which the Sceptic suspends judgement, i.e. the range of candidates for belief from which he withholds his assent, and (*b*) the contexts in which the Sceptic suspends judgement about these matters. The absence of insulation explains why, given that in the context of philosophical reflection the Sceptic suspends judgement about a certain range of matters, he suspends judgement about that same range of matters outside that context, that is, in the context of ordinary life. But the absence of insulation does not explain why the Sceptic suspends judgement about those matters about which he does suspend judgement in the context of philosophical reflection. That aspect of the scope of Scepticism can be explained only by appealing, as Sextus does, to the dogmatic distinction between the evident and the non-evident.

In drawing this distinction the dogmatic philosopher not only distinguishes two kinds of knowledge—inferential and non-inferential knowledge—but also claims about certain matters that they are evident (that is, things of which we do or can have non-inferential knowledge) and about other matters that they are non-evident (things of which we can have only inferential knowledge if we can have any knowledge of them at all). There are two ways in which Sextus uses the distinction between the evident and the non-evident to define the scope of Scepticism. First, Sextus uses this distinction to indicate that the Sceptic in philosophical reflection suspends judgement about all and only those matters the dogmatic philosopher regards either as evident or as non-evident. In claiming that it is evident that p the dogmatic philosopher claims that there is some criterion of truth K in virtue of which we do or can have non-inferential knowledge that p. The Sceptic's arguments against K or any criterion of truth of its kind are supposed to lead the Sceptic to suspend judgement about whether p.[39] But if the Sceptic suspends judgement about those matters the dogmatic philosopher regards as evident, and if according to the dogmatic philosopher we have knowledge of a non-evident matter, if we do, only on the basis of our knowledge of something he regards as an evident matter, then the Sceptic will also suspend judgement about all those matters the dogmatic philosopher regards as non-evident (see here especially *PH* 2.95 quoted above). The second way in which Sextus uses the distinction between the evident and the non-evident is to indicate that any matter about which the Sceptic suspends judgement has a certain status. For it is a matter about which suspension of judgement is, as it appears to the

---

[39] See especially *PH* 2.95 where, in view of his arguments against the kind of criterion of truth in virtue of which those matters the dogmatic philosopher regards as evident are supposed to be known, the Sceptic is said to be 'compelled to suspend judgement about what they [the dogmatic philosophers] call evident (ἐπέχειν περὶ τῶν ἐναργῶν καλουμένων ἀναγκαζώμεθα).' See also *M* 8.141 where these arguments are said to create 'an impasse over evident things (τὴν τῶν ἐναργῶν ἀπορίαν).' Cf. Barnes, 'The Beliefs of a Pyrrhonist', 76–8.

It is worth noting that the Sceptic has a variety of arguments on the basis of which he can come to suspend judgement about those matters the dogmatic philosopher regards as evident. According to the dogmatic philosopher an evident matter is something that can be directly observed. In claiming to suspend judgement about those matters the dogmatic philosopher regards as evident the Sceptic suspends judgement about those matters that, the dogmatic philosopher claims, we can directly observe. And the Sceptic can do so in view of e.g. arguments that purport to show that in sense perception we do not have direct access to, and so do not directly observe, the world (*M* 7.364–8, 8.357–60, 364–6), or (as in the Ten Modes) that we do not have sufficient reason to think that our sense perceptions of the world are reliable.

Sceptic, required. If the Sceptic suspends judgement about whether *p*, he does so because, as it appears to him, (1) it is non-evident whether *p* in the sense that one has reason to believe either *p* or its negation only if there is something evident to one that one takes to be a reason to believe either *p* or its negation, and (2) there is nothing evident to the Sceptic that he takes to be a reason to believe either *p* or its negation.

Now the claim that Sextus uses the distinction between the evident and the non-evident to define the scope of Scepticism is not especially informative. For it simply raises the question what it is a *dogmatic* belief is about in being about something *non-evident*. It seems to me that this question is best answered by considering what it is a *non-dogmatic* belief is about in being about something *evident*. Sextus tells us at *PH* 1.13 that the Sceptic assents to his own πάθη. If, as I have argued, the Sceptic assents only to what is evident to him, it follows that the Sceptic's own πάθη are evident to him. The fact that this is so explains, in turn, why according to Sextus at *PH* 1.13 the Sceptic does not deny having these πάθη.[40] A πάθος is a state or condition the Sceptic is in as the result of being affected by something else.[41] So to say, as Sextus does, that the Sceptic does not deny having the πάθη he has is just to say that for a range of conditions, if the Sceptic is in one of these conditions, he does not deny that this is so. Thus at *PH* 1.13 Sextus explains that if the Sceptic is in the condition of being warm (θερμαινόμενον) or cool (ψυχόμενος), he will not say 'I think I am not warm (or cool) (δοκῶ μὴ θερμαίνεσθαι ἢ ψύχεσθαι),' that is, he will not deny that he is warm or cool. A passage at *PH* 1.22 indicates that for Sextus its appearing to one that *p*, or an appearance that *p*, is a kind of πάθος. For he writes there that 'We say, then, that the criterion of the Sceptical way of life is what is apparent (τὸ φαινόμενον), implicitly meaning by this the appearance (φαντασία). For it [the appearance] consists in a passive and involuntary πάθος and is not an object of investigation (ἐν πείσει γὰρ καὶ ἀβουλήτῳ πάθει κειμένη ἀζήτητός ἐστιν).'[42] If, for example, it appears to the Sceptic that honey is sweet, then its appearing to him that honey is sweet is a πάθος the Sceptic has and so a condition he is in.

---

[40] Contrast Frede, 'The Sceptic's Beliefs', 20–1, who claims that 'assenting to an affection [= πάθος] does not consist in assuming that it exists'. His reasons for this claim, however, are obscure to me.

[41] More generally a πάθος is, as Brunschwig, 'Cyrenaic Epistemology', 252 explains, 'any effect produced on a patient by the action of an agent which affects it.'

[42] I follow Fine, 'Sceptical *Dogmatá*', 90–1 in translating ἐν . . . κειμένη as 'consists in' rather than, as Annas and Barnes, *Outlines*, do, 'depends on'. Fine is right in noting that for Sextus a φαντασία does not depend on, but rather is a kind of, πάθος.

If the Sceptic does not deny that he has this πάθος, and so does not deny that he is in this condition, then he does not deny that it appears to him that honey is sweet.

However, it does not follow from the fact that the Sceptic does not deny that it appears to him that honey is sweet that he *believes* that it appears to him that honey is sweet. It is possible to fail to deny *p* without believing *p*, and at *PH* 1.13 Sextus attributes to the Sceptic only the failure to deny, if he is warm or cool, that this is so. Yet if the Sceptic's own πάθη are evident to him, then the Sceptic has non-inferential knowledge of his own πάθη. And, as we have seen, an implication of Sextus' remarks at *PH* 1.215 on the differences between Scepticism and Cyrenaicism is that the Sceptic has this kind of knowledge of his own πάθη. If the Sceptic's πάθη include his appearances (φαντασίαι), as according to Sextus at *PH* 1.22 they do, then the Sceptic has non-inferential knowledge of his appearances. That is, if it appears to the Sceptic that *p*, then the Sceptic knows that it appears to him that *p*. If this is so, and if belief is a constituent of knowledge, then if it appears to the Sceptic that *p*, the Sceptic not only does not deny, but believes, that it appears to him that *p*.[43]

Moreover, at *PH* 1.22 Sextus says that an appearance, as a kind of πάθος, is *not* an object of investigation (it is ἀζήτητος). This is so because the Sceptic's own πάθη are evident to him, that is, he has non-inferential knowledge of his own πάθη. The object of any investigation, and so that about which it is possible to suspend judgement, is something non-evident—something that can be known, if it can be known at all, only on the basis of an inference from something else that is known. At *PH* 1.19–20 Sextus writes that

When we investigate whether existing things are such as they appear, we grant that they appear (ὅτι φαίνεται δίδομεν), and what we investigate is not what is apparent

---

[43] I reject the claim by Barnes, 'The Beliefs of a Pyrrhonist', 65–6, that the Sceptic's utterance of a sentence of the form 'it appears to me that *p*' is an 'avowal' or 'confession' rather than a statement, and so does not express any belief about how things appear to the Sceptic to be. (Barnes's claim is accepted by Hankinson, *The Sceptics*, 295, and similar claims are to be found in Stough, 'Sextus Empiricus on Non-Assertion', 140–1 and McPherran, 'Skeptical Homeopathy and Self-Refutation', 294–7.) As far as I can see the contrast Barnes draws between 'avowals' or 'confessions' and statements is to be found nowhere in Sextus' text. It is true that in several passages Sextus tells us that the Sceptic in uttering a sceptical phrase (σκεπτικὴ φωνή) 'reports' (ἀπαγγέλλει) his πάθος, but in each of these passages (*PH* 1.4, 1.15, 1.197, 1.200, 1.203) the Sceptic's reporting his πάθος consists in his making a statement about how things appear to him to be rather than a statement about how things are.

(τοῦ φαινομένου) but what is said about what is apparent—and this is different from investigating what is apparent itself. For example, it appears to us that honey sweetens (φαίνεται ἡμῖν γλυκάζειν τὸ μέλι). We concede (συγχωροῦμεν) this— for we are sweetened in a perceptual way. But we investigate whether, as far as the argument goes, it is sweet. And this is not what is apparent (τὸ φαινόμενον) but something said about what is apparent.

According to Sextus here it is non-evident to the Sceptic, and so something the Sceptic investigates and comes to suspend judgement about, whether the honey *is* sweet. The Sceptic does not investigate whether it *appears* to him that the honey is sweet. And the best explanation for why this is so is that it is evident to the Sceptic, and so the Sceptic has non-inferential knowledge, that it appears to him that the honey is sweet.

So, in summary, Sextus' remarks at *PH* 1.13 on the scope of Scepticism are to be understood in the following way. The Sceptic assents to his own πάθη. The fact that he does so is supposed to explain the fact that the Sceptic does not deny that he has beliefs in one sense of 'belief', namely, the sense in which a belief is a matter of 'acquiescing in something' (τὸ εὐδοκεῖν τινι). But the first fact can explain the second only if assenting to one's own πάθη is sufficient for having a belief in the sense of 'acquiescing in something'. But what is it to have a belief in this sense? Sextus in *PH* 1.13 does not answer this question explicitly, but he does so by implication. For he says that the Sceptic does not have beliefs in the sense of 'belief' in which belief is assent to something non-evident. But, as Sextus indicates elsewhere, assent is given to something non-evident only if that assent is the product of an inference. So in claiming, as Sextus does in *PH* 1.13, that the Sceptic does not assent to anything non-evident, Sextus is claiming that the Sceptic does not make any inferences.[44] *A fortiori* the Sceptic does not have any belief that is the product of an inference. Since the distinction between the evident and the non-evident is exhaustive, and since the Sceptic does not assent to anything non-evident, it follows that if the Sceptic assents to something, he assents to something evident. But, Sextus tells us at *PH* 1.13,

---

[44] In fact there are two passages in Sextus—*PH* 2.102 and *M* 8.156–8—that call into question the claim that the Sceptic does not make inferences. These are the passages where Sextus, surprisingly, says that the Sceptic does *not* suspend judgement about, and even makes use of, the so-called recollective (ὑπομνηστικόν) sign. I have nothing illuminating to say about these mystifying passages. For a useful discussion of the problems they present, see Allen, *Inference from Signs*, 115–22. Cf. also Mates, *The Skeptic Way*, 275.

the Sceptic does assent to something: he assents to his own πάθη. It follows, then, that the Sceptic's own πάθη are evident to him. But to say this is, in virtue of what it means for something to be evident, just to say that the Sceptic has knowledge of, and so beliefs about, his own πάθη where these beliefs are *not* the products of an inference. Since, as Sextus indicates at *PH* 1.22, an appearance is a kind of πάθος, the Sceptic's beliefs about his own πάθη include beliefs about how things appear to him to be. If this is right, then for Sextus a non-dogmatic belief is a belief about how things appear to one to be. A dogmatic belief—the kind of belief the Sceptic, in virtue of being a Sceptic, lacks—is any belief about how things *are* rather than merely *appear* to one to be.

At *PH* 1.19, and referring back to *PH* 1.13, Sextus writes: 'As we said before, we do not overturn anything which leads us to assent involuntarily in accordance with a passive appearance—and these are what is apparent.'[45] Here, as at *PH* 1.13, Sextus describes the Sceptic as assenting not to but 'in accordance with' (κατά) an appearance (φαντασία). But what is the difference between assenting *to* an appearance and assenting *in accordance with* that appearance? I take it that it is the difference between assenting to the *content* of an appearance—e.g. that honey is sweet, that the tower is round, the virtue is knowledge—and assenting to the fact that one has an appearance with this content.[46] So when the Sceptic assents 'in accordance with' his appearance that honey is sweet he assents to, and comes to believe, not that the honey is sweet but that it appears to him that honey is sweet. It is important, too, that at *PH* 1.19 Sextus describes the appearance 'in accordance with' which the Sceptic assents as 'passive' (παθητικήν). For to say of an appearance that it is passive is to say that the appearance is a πάθος. If an appearance is a πάθος, then to believe that one has an appearance with a certain content is to believe that one has a certain πάθος and so that one is in a certain condition. In this way Sextus' talk at *PH* 1.19 of assenting 'in accordance with' a passive appearance is equivalent to his talk at *PH* 1.13 of assenting to πάθη.

In this chapter I have argued that, according to Sextus, the scope of Scepticism is restricted in the following way. Although the Sceptic, in virtue of being a Sceptic, has no beliefs about how things *are*, he does have beliefs about how things *appear* to him to be. Understood in this

---

[45] τὰ γὰρ κατὰ φαντασίαν παθητικὴν ἀβουλήτως ἡμᾶς ἄγοντα εἰς συγκατάθεσιν οὐκ ἀνατρέπομεν, ὡς καὶ ἔμπροσθεν ἐλέγομεν· ταῦτα δέ ἐστι τὰ φαινόμενα.

[46] Here I disagree with Barney, 'Appearances and Impressions', 300–1.

way the scope of Scepticism raises a set of questions about the *viability* of Scepticism. For Sextus presents Scepticism as a way of life that, as it appears to the Sceptic, delivers more tranquillity than any other for the person who follows it. But how, if it requires that one not have any beliefs about how things *are*, can Scepticism be a possible, let alone desirable, way of life? How can someone who lacks any belief about how things are, as the Sceptic claims he does, *act* or *do* anything at all? That is the question I take up in the next chapter.

4

Appearances and Action

Sextus presents Scepticism as a kind of philosophy but also, and no less, as a possible way of life. And since antiquity the claim that Scepticism is a possible way of life has seemed especially suspect. For the Sceptic can live only if his Scepticism permits him to act. Yet, it is claimed, there is a feature of Scepticism as Sextus describes it—a feature that makes Scepticism the kind of philosophy and the way of life Sextus says it is—that is incompatible with action or activity of any sort. *This* claim is the *apraxia* or inaction objection to Scepticism.

There are a number of different but equivalent formulations of the *apraxia* objection. This is so because there are different ways of describing that feature of Scepticism that is supposed to be incompatible with action.[1] We can formulate the *apraxia* objection as the claim that the Sceptic cannot act because he suspends judgement about everything. But the Sceptic does *not* suspend judgement about everything in the sense that he has no beliefs at all. For, as I argued in Chapter 3, it is clear from *PH* 1.13 that according to Sextus the Sceptic has some beliefs. These are beliefs of the kind I called *non-dogmatic*. The Sceptic suspends judgement about everything in the sense that he lacks *all* beliefs of some other kind—all *dogmatic* beliefs. So the formulation of the *apraxia* objection in terms of the Sceptic's suspension of judgement is equivalent to its formulation as the claim that the Sceptic cannot act because he has no dogmatic beliefs. Each of these formulations, in turn, is equivalent to a formulation of the *apraxia* objection in terms of the kind of assent the Sceptic withholds universally. Sextus at *PH* 1.13 tells us that there are some things to which the Sceptic assents, and he indicates there that by assenting to these things the Sceptic acquires non-dogmatic beliefs. Call the kind of assent the Sceptic gives to some things *non-dogmatic* assent and the kind of assent he withholds universally—the kind of assent that

[1] In thinking about this issue I have benefited from reading Katja Vogt's unpublished paper 'Activity, Action, and Assent'.

yields dogmatic beliefs—*dogmatic* assent. We can formulate the *apraxia* objection as the claim that the Sceptic cannot act because he fails to give dogmatic assent to anything. But the Sceptic fails to give dogmatic assent to anything just insofar as he suspends judgement about everything in the sense that he has no dogmatic beliefs. So the formulation of the *apraxia* objection in terms of the Sceptic's failure to give dogmatic assent to anything is equivalent to its formulations in terms of the Sceptic's suspension of judgement about everything or his lack of dogmatic beliefs.

Of course *by itself* none of these formulations of the *apraxia* objection is informative. The *apraxia* objection claims that Scepticism has a certain feature and that this feature of Scepticism is incompatible with action or activity of any sort. But the *apraxia* objection misses its target unless the feature of Scepticism it claims is incompatible with action or activity of any kind is in fact a feature of Scepticism *as Sextus describes it.* A proponent of the *apraxia* objection must start from a correct understanding of what, according to Sextus, Scepticism is, and he must then argue that Scepticism so understood is not a possible way of life because Scepticism so understood has some feature that is incompatible with action. This feature is the Sceptic's suspension of judgement about everything where that is the same thing as the Sceptic's failure to give dogmatic assent to anything where that, in turn, is the same thing as the Sceptic's lack of dogmatic beliefs. But to claim, as the *apraxia* objection does, that the Sceptic cannot act because—to use just one of several equivalent formulations—he lacks dogmatic beliefs is to claim that dogmatic belief is required for action. But, again, the *apraxia* objection misses its target unless the kind of belief it claims is required for action is the kind of belief—dogmatic belief—Sextus himself says is absent from the Sceptic's life. So we will understand what it is the *apraxia* objection claims is required for action, and so what it is whose absence from the Sceptic's life is supposed to render the Sceptic incapable of action, only if we understand what, according to Sextus, dogmatic belief is and how it is different from non-dogmatic belief. In this way an adequate interpretation of the content of the *apraxia* objection, and of Sextus' response to the objection, must include, or at least presuppose, an interpretation of the scope of Scepticism.

In Chapter 3 I argued that, according to Sextus, dogmatic belief—belief of the kind the Sceptic, in virtue of his Scepticism, lacks—is belief about how things *are* rather than merely *appear* to one to be. If this is right, then the *apraxia* argument misses its target unless it is understood as the claim that the Sceptic cannot act because he lacks beliefs about how things are rather than merely appear to him to be. This claim, in turn, can be expanded into the following argument. Action requires beliefs about how things are. Therefore, if the Sceptic does not have any beliefs of this kind, then he cannot act. Yet if the Sceptic's Scepticism prevents him from acting, then Scepticism is not, as Sextus claims it is, a possible way of life. If, alternatively, the Sceptic does act, then he has beliefs about how things are and is not, after all, a Sceptic. This is, in its general form, the *apraxia* or inaction argument against Scepticism, and its conclusion is that Scepticism is incompatible with action.[2]

Hume in a celebrated passage from *An Enquiry Concerning Human Understanding* writes:

[A] ... [a Pyrrhonian] must acknowledge, if he will acknowledge any thing, that all human life must perish, were his principles universally and steadily to prevail. All discourse, all action would immediately cease; and men remain in a total lethargy, till the necessities of nature, unsatisfied, put an end to their miserable existence. [B] It is true; so fatal an event is very little to be dreaded. Nature is always too strong for principle. And though a PYRRHONIAN may throw himself or others into a momentary amazement and confusion by his profound reasonings; the first and most trivial event in life will put to flight all his doubts and scruples, and leave him the same, in every point of action and speculation, with the philosophers of every other sect, or with those who never concerned themselves in any philosophical researches. When he awakes from his dream, he will be the first to join in the laugh against himself, and to confess, that all his objections are mere amusement, and can have no other tendency than to show the whimsical condition of mankind, who must act and reason and believe; though they are not able, by their most diligent enquiry, to satisfy themselves concerning the foundation of these operations, or to remove the objections, which may be raised against them.[3]

---

[2] Striker, 'Sceptical Strategies', 100–4 distinguishes two versions of the *apraxia* argument advanced by the Stoics against the Academics. One version argues that if knowledge is impossible (that is, if there are no cognitive impressions), then it is not possible *to decide* how to act; the other version argues that if a person were to suspend judgement about everything (if a person were to divest herself of all beliefs), it would not be possible for her to act. Sextus does not respond to the first of these two versions of the *apraxia* argument. He may fail to do so because he is not aware of it or does not distinguish it from the second version of the *apraxia* argument. Or, more charitably, he does not respond to it because he, or the Sceptic he describes, is not its target. For the first version of the *apraxia* argument targets someone who claims, as the Sceptic does not, that nothing can be known.

[3] Hume, *An Enquiry Concerning Human Understanding*, 12.23. I have divided the passage into two parts, (A) and (B).

Hume here offers not one but two arguments against Scepticism.[4] In part (A) of the passage Hume argues that if a person were to do what the Sceptic claims to do and divest himself of all belief, then he would be incapable of action. This is the *apraxia* argument, and its suppressed premiss is that action requires belief. In part (B) Hume argues that it is not possible for a human being to do what the Sceptic claims to do, namely, to divest himself of all belief. This argument is *not* the *apraxia* argument. For it takes as its starting point the claim that a human being has beliefs—beliefs about how things are—as a matter of natural necessity. According to this argument—which we might call *the natural necessity argument* against Scepticism—it is certain facts about a human being's natural belief-forming mechanisms, and not the conditions of action, that make a life without beliefs of the kind the Sceptic claims to lack impossible. Hume insists that while the Sceptic's arguments expose the unreasonableness of certain beliefs, we cannot abandon, as the Sceptic claims to do, those beliefs whose unreasonableness these arguments expose. That is the sense in which, as Hume says, 'Nature is always too strong for principle.' Yet if it is not possible for a human being to divest himself of all belief, then it is an idle question whether belief is required for action. For that question is now the question whether, *per impossibile*, a person were to divest himself of all belief, he would be able to act.[5] This question is idle in the sense that an affirmative answer to it does not compromise the natural necessity argument against Scepticism.

The Sceptic can reply to the natural necessity argument only by arguing against the view of human nature according to which beliefs of the kind the Sceptic claims to live without are naturally necessary. And the Sceptic can reply to the *apraxia* argument only by arguing that action does *not* require beliefs of the kind the Sceptic, in virtue of his Scepticism, lacks. In making *this* argument it is plausible to think of the Sceptic as doing several things at once. First, he is following a certain dialectical strategy.[6] The Sceptic's argument for the claim that action does not require belief about how things are counters his critic's argument for

---

[4] This point is missed by Johnsen, 'On the Coherence of Pyrrhonian Skepticism', 524–5. Johnsen correctly notes, however, that Frede, 'The Sceptic's Beliefs', 2 mischaracterizes the *apraxia* argument as purporting to show that Scepticism is self-refuting or inconsistent.

[5] See the useful remarks in Johnsen, 'On the Coherence of Pyrrhonian Skepticism', 560–1.

[6] Cf. Frede, 'The Sceptic's Beliefs', 6.

the claim that action does require belief of this kind, and by doing so is supposed to render the latter claim (as well, of course, as the former) something about which one is rationally required to suspend judgement. If, as the result of his argument for the claim that action does not require belief about how things are, the Sceptic succeeds in arguing that there is no reason to believe that action requires belief of this kind, then the Sceptic has undermined the *apraxia* argument. For if there is no reason to believe that action requires belief about how things are, then there is no reason to believe that the Sceptic cannot act, and that Scepticism is not viable, *because* the Sceptic does not have beliefs of this kind. The most the Sceptic's critic can argue for is the conditional claim that *if* action does require belief about how things are, then the Sceptic cannot act and Scepticism is not viable. But by itself the truth of that conditional conclusion poses no threat to Scepticism.[7]

Second, the Sceptic himself suspends judgement about whether or not action requires belief about how things are, and he does so in part on the basis of his argument that action does not require belief of this kind. Nonetheless, in making this argument the Sceptic is reporting that it *appears* to him that action does not require belief about how things are. But, third, he is also reporting that it appears to him that there is a reason why it appears to him that action does not require belief about

---

[7] This is not the only dialectical strategy available to Sextus. For it is possible for Sextus to follow a strategy that consists in showing that his opponent, the dogmatic philosopher, is committed to a certain claim in virtue of being committed to certain other claims. So in replying to the *apraxia* argument Sextus argues that action does not require belief about how things are. If in doing so he were following a dialectical strategy of this sort, he would be arguing that the dogmatic philosopher who advances the *apraxia* argument is, in virtue of his commitment to certain other philosophical claims, committed to the claim that action does *not* require belief about how things are. If successful, this dialectical strategy reveals that in advancing the *apraxia* argument the dogmatic philosopher is making a claim—that action requires belief about how things are—that is inconsistent with other claims he accepts as true. Note, however, that this dialectical strategy cannot succeed in answering the *apraxia* argument simply by revealing, if it does, that the dogmatic philosopher who makes it is being inconsistent in making it. The dogmatic philosopher can remove the inconsistency this dialectical strategy has revealed by continuing to advance the *apraxia* argument while abandoning those claims the strategy has shown to be inconsistent with it. So if Sextus were to follow this strategy, he would not only have to show that the dogmatic philosopher is inconsistent in making the *apraxia* argument, but he would have to do so in a way that leads the dogmatic philosopher to reject as false, or at least to suspend judgement about, the claim that is the core of the *apraxia* argument, namely, that action requires belief about how things are. For, obviously, once the dogmatic philosopher rejects this claim as false, or at least suspends judgement about it, he can no longer advance the *apraxia* argument against Scepticism.

how things are. So the Sceptic is reporting not only (*a*) that it appears to him that action does not require belief about how things are, but also (*b*) that it appears to him that the reason this is so is that it appears to him that each of the premisses of his argument for the conclusion that action does not require belief of this kind is true *and* it appears to him that the conclusion of the argument follows from its premisses.[8] Just as it can (and does) appear to the Sceptic that action does not require belief about how things are, so it can (and does) appear to the Sceptic that there is a reason why this appears to him to be so. Further, it can (and does) appear to the Sceptic that the reason why it appears to him that action does not require belief about how things are is that it appears to him that *p* and it appears to him that *q* and it appears to him that it follows from *p* and *q* that action does not require belief of this kind.

There are two ways in which Sextus can argue that action does not require beliefs of the kind the Sceptic, in virtue of his Scepticism, lacks. For he can argue *either* that action does not require beliefs of *any* kind, *or* that action requires only beliefs of the kind Scepticism permits the Sceptic to have.[9] Sextus argues in the first rather than the second way. Though the Sceptic as Sextus describes him has beliefs about how things appear to him to be, Sextus does not argue that these beliefs are sufficient for action in the absence of beliefs about how things are. And he is right not to do so. For the *apraxia* argument turns on the claim that action requires belief about how things are, and there is a persuasive line of thought in support of that claim. It is that action, at a minimum, is a matter of an agent attempting to satisfy some desire she has. But an agent cannot so much as attempt to satisfy a desire she has,

---

[8] Here I follow Johnsen, 'On the Coherence of Pyrrhonian Skepticism', 538–9.

[9] The two argumentative strategies available to the Sceptic correspond to the two general strategies the Academics appear to have identified for responding to the *apraxia* argument. The first strategy is to argue that action does not require assent and that impressions by themselves—that is, apart from any kind of assent given to them—are sufficient for action. This is at least one of the strategies Arcesilaus seems to have adopted. See Plutarch, *Against Colotes* 1122B–D. The second strategy is to argue that there is a kind of assent that is compatible with the Academics' universal suspension of judgement and this kind of assent is sufficient for action. This appears to have been Carneades' principle strategy in responding to the *apraxia* argument by offering the doctrine of the πιθανόν. The first strategy is not an especially successful one for the Academics. For if, as the Stoics claim, human action is distinguished from mere animal behaviour by the fact that it is, while animal behaviour is not, caused by assent, the first strategy erases the distinction between human action and animal behaviour. Since the Stoics were strongly committed to this distinction, the first strategy has limited dialectical value as a response to the Stoics' *apraxia* argument. For this point see Striker, 'Sceptical Strategies', 104, and Obrdzalek, 'Living in Doubt: Carneades' *Pithanon* Reconsidered', 257–8.

let alone succeed in satisfying it, if she does not have some belief about *how* to satisfy it. And having a belief about how to satisfy a desire requires having beliefs about how things *are*—how the world is now, how the world must change in order for the desire to be satisfied, and how this change is to be made. Beliefs of the sort the Sceptic claims to lack—beliefs about how things are—*guide* an agent in action, that is, in attempting to satisfy some desire she has. By itself no belief about how things merely appear to one to be can provide this kind of guidance. Suppose I desire to do *x* and it appears to me, but I do not believe, that I can do *x* only by doing *y*. In believing that it appears to me that I can do *x* only by doing *y* I do not believe anything about how to satisfy my desire to do *x*. I believe only something about myself, namely, that I am in a certain psychological state or condition—what Sextus calls a πάθος—in which it appears to me that I can do *x* only by doing *y*. Sextus argues that a psychological state or condition of this kind, and not the belief that one is in it, makes action possible for the Sceptic by guiding the Sceptic in action.

The Sceptic can argue that action does not require belief of *any* kind only by arguing that something other than belief is sufficient for action. This is what Sextus does. At *PH* 1.21 he writes:

That we attend to what is apparent (τοῖς φαινομένοις προσέχομεν) is clear from what we say about the criterion of the Sceptical way of life (τοῦ κριτηρίου τῆς σκεπτικῆς ἀγωγῆς). 'Criterion' has two senses: the criterion adopted to provide conviction about the reality or unreality of something (we shall discuss these criteria when we turn to attack them); and the criterion of action, attending to which in everyday life we perform some actions and not others (τό τε τοῦ πράσσειν, ᾧ προσέχοντες κατὰ τὸν βίον τὰ μὲν πράσσομεν τὰ δ' οὔ).

According to Sextus here the Sceptic has a criterion (κριτήριον) of action. A criterion of action is something that explains the Sceptic's actions. The fact that the Sceptic has a criterion of action is supposed to explain why he is active rather than inactive, that is, why he does something rather than nothing. Thus Sextus elsewhere writes that the Sceptic must have a criterion of action 'so as not to be completely inactive and without any part in the affairs of life' (*M* 7.30). And the criterion of action the Sceptic has is supposed to explain why he acts as he does, that is, why he performs some actions and not others.[10] Sextus continues (*PH* 1.22):

---

[10] Cf. Barnes, 'Pyrrhonism, Belief, and Causation', 2642.

we say, then, that the criterion of the Sceptic way of life is what is apparent (τὸ φαινόμενον), implicitly meaning by this the appearance (τὴν φαντασίαν). For it [the appearance] consists in a passive and involuntary condition and is not an object of investigation (ἐν πείσει γὰρ καὶ ἀβουλήτῳ πάθει κειμένη ἀζήτητός ἐστιν).

Sextus identifies the Sceptic's criterion of action with a psychological state or condition (a πάθος) that has content but is not a belief. It is instead the state or condition in which it appears to one that *p*. Call this state or condition an *appearance*.[11] In saying that the Sceptic's criterion of action is an appearance Sextus is making two claims. He is claiming, first, than an appearance can *guide* action. This, I take it, is the import of his remark that when the Sceptic acts, and when he performs one action rather than another, he 'attends' (προσέχει) to an appearance.[12] Second, Sextus is claiming that attending to an appearance that *p* in a way that allows that appearance to guide one's action is different from, and does not require, assenting to that appearance and having the belief that *p*. Now if the Sceptic has an appearance that *p*, then it appears to him that *p* and, as I argued in Chapter 3, he believes that it appears to him that *p*. According to Sextus, however, it is the appearance that *p*, and not the

---

[11] At *PH* 1.22 Sextus explains that he is using the term τὸ φαινόμενον ('what is apparent') as a synonym for ἡ φαντασία (the appearance).

The formulations 'it appears that *p*' or 'the appearance that *p*' suggest that the πάθος Sextus calls τὸ φαινόμενον or ἡ φαντασία can be described in a way that does not imply the existence of any object in the world (besides, of course, the subject of the πάθος). Describing a πάθος as its appearing to me that honey is sweet or as the appearance that honey is sweet does not imply the existence of honey or anything else. But this same πάθος might also be described as the honey's appearing sweet to me or as the appearance of the honey as sweet to me. So we have these possible descriptions of the πάθος that is supposed to be the Sceptic's criterion of action.

(1) its appearing to me that *x* is *F*.
(2) the appearance that *x* is *F*.
(1*) *x*'s appearing *F* to me.
(2*) the appearance of *x* as *F* to me.

Sextus' remark at *PH* 1.22 that 'no one, presumably, will raise a controversy over whether an existing thing appears this way or that (περὶ μὲν τοῦ φαίνεσθαι τοῖον ἢ τοῖον τὸ ὑποκείμενον); rather, they investigate whether it is such as it appears' suggest that he has in view descriptions of the form (1*) and (2*). But this is not always the case, and as far as I can see Sextus does not clearly or consistently distinguish (1) and (2) from (1*) and (2*). For discussion of this matter, and of the related question whether the Sceptic entertains, accepts, or is committed to some form of 'external world' scepticism, see Burnyeat, 'Idealism and Greek Philosophy: What Descartes Saw and Berkeley Missed', 29–30; Everson, 'The Objective Appearance of Pyrrhonism', 136–7; Hankinson, *The Sceptics*, 25–6; and especially Fine, 'Sextus and External World Scepticism', 349–52.

[12] See also D.L. 9.106 where Aenesidemus is reported to have said that Pyrrho 'follows what is apparent' (τοῖς φαινομένοις ἀκολουθεῖν).

Sceptic's belief that it appears to him that *p*, that guides the Sceptic in action. Sextus at *PH* 1.13 admits beliefs of a certain kind into the Sceptic's life—beliefs about how things appear to one to be—but it is a mistake to think that according to Sextus beliefs of this kind guide the Sceptic in action and so make it possible for the Sceptic to be active.

At *PH* 1.22 Sextus tells us that the reason why the Sceptic's appearances are his criterion of action is that an appearance is *not* an object of investigation.[13] To say that an appearance the Sceptic has is not an object of investigation is just to say that the existence of this appearance, or whether or not he has this appearance, is not something about which the Sceptic suspends judgement. If the Sceptic has an appearance that *p*, it is evident to him that this is so, that is, it is evident to him that it appears to him that *p* and so that he has an appearance that *p*. In this important respect the status of the Sceptic's criterion of *action* is, according to Sextus, different from the status of the dogmatic philosopher's criterion of *truth*. For Sextus argues (*PH* 2.18–21) that the existence of a criterion of truth (e.g. the Stoics' 'cognitive impression' (καταληπτικὴ φαντασία)) *is* something about which we are rationally required to suspend judgement, and so is something about which the Sceptic does suspend judgement.

At *PH* 1.23–24 Sextus writes:

Attending to what is apparent, then, we live in accordance with the ordinary regimen of life, without holding beliefs—for we cannot be utterly inactive (τοῖς φαινομένοις οὖν προσέχοντες κατὰ τὴν βιωτικὴν τήρησιν ἀδοξάστως βιοῦμεν, ἐπεὶ μὴ δυνάμεθα ἀνενέργητοι παντάπασιν εἶναι). This ordinary regimen of life seems to have four parts, and to consist in guidance by nature (ὑφήγησις φύσεως), the necessity of conditions (ἀνάγκη παθῶν), the handing down of laws and customs, and teaching of kinds of expertise. By nature's guidance we are naturally capable of perceiving and thinking (φυσικῶς αἰσθητικοὶ καὶ νοητικοί ἐσμεν). By the necessity of conditions, hunger guides us to food and thirst to drink. By the handing down of customs and laws, we accept in the conduct of life (παραλαμβάνομεν βιωτικῶς) that piety is good and impiety bad. By teaching of kinds of expertise we are not inactive in those which we accept. And we say all this without holding beliefs.

According to Sextus there are various ways in which attending to appearances enables the Sceptic to participate in—that is, to live a life that instantiates—the ordinary regimen of life. For my purposes here two points are especially important in connection with this passage. First, Sextus says that nature guides a human being in living her life and

---

[13] As Sextus' use of the inferential particle γάρ indicates.

it does so through a human being's *natural* capacities for perception and thought. I take it—though, to be sure, Sextus' text is cryptic—that Sextus is arguing that the exercise of these capacities can and normally does, but in fact need not, involve the acquisition of beliefs about how things are. The Sceptic exercises these natural capacities, and is thereby guided by nature in living his life, insofar as he has both perceptual and non-perceptual appearances (and, perhaps, experiences associative connections among his appearances).[14] On this line of thought, the dogmatic philosopher is wrong in thinking that it is *natural*—in the sense of naturally *necessary*—for a human being to have beliefs and that this is so because nature can guide a human being in living her life only by endowing her with beliefs. For it is not beliefs but appearances that a human being must have as a matter of natural necessity; and it is not only beliefs, but also appearances, through which nature can guide a human being in living her life.[15]

Second, the ordinary regimen of life includes having and satisfying certain basic desires—what Sextus calls 'the necessity of conditions' (ἀνάγκη παθῶν). The necessity to which Sextus refers is the necessity that connects the presence of these desires with the actions by which they are satisfied, e.g. hunger is necessarily connected with eating, and thirst with drinking. Now Sextus implies something he does not explicitly state, namely, that when the Sceptic eats as a result of being hungry he does so without beliefs about how things are. The context of the passage makes this implication clear. For Sextus is explaining how the Sceptic lives in accordance with the ordinary regimen of life without having those beliefs that fall within the scope of his Scepticism—how, as Sextus says at *PH* 1.23, the Sceptic lives an ordinary life ἀδοξάστως. But it is a mistake to think that in claiming that hunger 'guides' (ὁδηγεῖ) the Sceptic to eat, and does so in the absence of beliefs, that Sextus is claiming that at least in the Sceptic's case the desire that is hunger is sufficient for the action of eating and by itself explains why the Sceptic eats. We need to distinguish here the claim that the Sceptic's eating can

---

[14] Cf. Mates, *The Skeptic Way*, 231. Barnes, 'Pyrrhonism, Belief, and Causation', 2646–9 connects 'guidance by nature' (ὑφήγησις φύσεως) with Sextus' discussion of recollective signs at *PH* 2.100–2. On one reading of that discussion—though, as Barnes notes, not necessarily the most plausible reading of it—Sextus is claiming that the Sceptic, like anyone else, experiences associative connections among his appearances.

[15] For a different interpretation of Sextus' claim that by nature's guidance the Sceptic can perceive and think—an interpretation according to which Sextus, in making the claim, exploits certain dogmatic philosophical theories of concept formation to explain how the Sceptic can think and inquire—see Vogt, *Skepsis und Lebenspraxis*, 159–60.

be explained without attributing to the Sceptic beliefs about how things are from the claim that the Sceptic's eating can be explained by attributing to the Sceptic *only* a desire for food.[16] Sextus' claim is that the Sceptic, by attending to appearances, eats when he is hungry: the Sceptic's desire for food, together with the relevant appearance to which he attends, explains why he eats and why he eats what he does eat.

Conditions like thirst and hunger are among the basic desires that explain in part a wide range of actions people ordinarily perform. It is not easy to see how Sextus could argue that the Sceptic performs actions in this range and yet lacks these desires. And so Sextus does not deny that the Sceptic has basic desires like hunger and thirst. At *PH* 1.29 he writes that 'We do not, however, take the Sceptics to be undisturbed in every way (ἀόχλητον πάντῃ); for we agree that at times they shiver and are thirsty and are in other conditions of this kind.' Sextus argues that the Sceptic, in virtue of his Scepticism, enjoys more tranquillity than anyone else. But, as Sextus concedes here, the Sceptic's tranquillity is not complete. For the Sceptic, no less than anyone else, is subject to a certain kind of distress, and this is so because the Sceptic, no less than anyone else, is a creature with a body. As a result the Sceptic, no less than anyone else, is subject to bodily conditions, and some of these bodily conditions are sources of distress. And that is so because some of these bodily conditions are desires, like thirst and hunger, that can and at least sometimes do go unsatisfied.[17]

So here, in summary, is what I take to be the substance of Sextus' reply to the *apraxia* argument. The Sceptic has no beliefs about how things are, but he has (and cannot avoid having) appearances, and these appearances, together with his desires, are sufficient for action. The explanation of any action the Sceptic performs will have the form '*S* does action *A* because he desires to ϕ and it appears to him that *p*' where *p* is, typically, a complex proposition that relates the doing of *A* to ϕ-ing and so to the satisfaction of the desire to ϕ. For example, the Sceptic drinks a glass of water because he is thirsty, i.e. has a desire to drink, and it appears to the Sceptic that there is a glass of water in front of him and that he can drink it. The appearance to which the explanation of the Sceptic's action appeals is not a belief, but it is an analogue to belief in the sense that it plays the role in the explanation of the Sceptic's actions that belief plays

---

[16] As, it seems to me, Barnes, 'Pyrrhonism, Belief, and Causation', 2642–3 and n. 139 fails to do.

[17] Cf. McPherran, '*Ataraxia* and *Eudaimonia* in Ancient Pyrrhonism', 153.

in the explanation of the non-Sceptic's actions. Moreover, Sextus seems to place no restriction on the actions the Sceptic can perform. For *any* action A, if the explanation of the non-Sceptic's performance of A appeals to the belief that *p*, the explanation of the Sceptic's performance of A appeals to the appearance that *p*. Thus, as Sextus indicates at *PH* 1.23–4, the Sceptic can perform not only simple actions like eating and drinking, but also the far more complex actions that constitute the practice of a technical skill or expertise (a τέχνη) like medicine.[18] So by arguing that appearances, together with desires, are sufficient for action, Sextus can argue that action does not require belief about how things are.

The first point point to make in assessing Sextus' reply to the *apraxia* argument is that even as a mere outline of a reply it is incomplete. Sextus argues that an appearance (in conjunction with a desire) is sufficient for action because appearances, like beliefs, can guide action. Sextus makes this argument, however, without explaining how an appearance is different from a belief. As the Sceptic's criterion of action, an appearance is simply a psychological state that can play the same role in the explanation of action as belief. If this is so, however, the dogmatic philosopher who makes the *apraxia* argument against Scepticism can object that since it plays the same explanatory role as belief, an appearance just *is* a belief and living by appearances, as the Sceptic claims to do, just is a matter of having and acting upon beliefs.[19] So Sextus' reply is incomplete until he provides some account of how an appearance is different from a belief. Recall that Sextus replies to the *apraxia* argument by arguing that action does not require belief of *any* kind. Sextus can do this, in turn, only by arguing that something other than belief, namely appearance, is (in conjunction with desire) sufficient for action. But, I am now claiming, Sextus can make *this* argument only if he can provide an account of the difference between an appearance and a belief.

Assume for the sake of simplicity that there is a single feature of belief in virtue of which it is capable of guiding action in the way that it does. Call this feature *the action-guiding feature* of belief. It is plausible to think that if any psychological state other than belief can guide action, it is because this psychological state, too, has the action-guiding feature belief has. So if, as Sextus claims, an appearance can guide action, then in at least one

---

[18] Cf. Barnes, 'Pyrrhonism, Belief, and Causation', 2644–6; Burnyeat, 'Can the Sceptic Live his Scepticism?', 37–8 and n. 26; and McPherran, '*Ataraxia* and *Eudaimonia* in Ancient Pyrrhonism', 160–5.

[19] See Annas, *The Morality of Happiness*, 211 and 357–8.

important respect an appearance is, and must be, similar to a belief. For an
appearance has, and must have, the same action-guiding feature as a belief.
But if, as Sextus' reply to the *apraxia* argument requires, an appearance has
the same action-guiding feature as a belief, then Sextus can provide an
account of how an appearance is different from a belief only by identifying
that feature that, in addition to the action-guiding feature, a psychological
state must have in order to be a belief. Call this feature *the belief-making
feature* of a belief. (Assume, again, for the sake of simplicity that there is a
single feature in virtue of which a psychological state is a belief.) Sextus can
distinguish an appearance from a belief only by arguing that an appearance
lacks the belief-making feature of a belief. In this way Sextus' reply to the
apraxia argument must include an account of what the belief-making
feature of a belief is, that is, an account of what it is that makes a
psychological state a belief.

There is an additional problem for Sextus in arguing that appearances, together with desires, are sufficient for action. At first glance the
appearance that *p* is similar to the belief that *p* only with respect to its
content: the appearance that *p*, like the belief that *p*, is a psychological
state that has the proposition *p* as its content. Now it is not the
propositional content of a psychological state that makes that psychological state a belief. A belief is only one among many psychological
states that can have a given proposition as its content: I can believe that
p, but I can also (for example) imagine, suppose, desire, or fear that *p*. So
the one feature it is clear an appearance has in common with a belief—
the possession of propositional content—is not what I have called the
belief-making feature of a belief. The problem for Sextus, however, is
that for all he has told us the possession of propositional content is the
only feature an appearance has. Yet the possession of propositional
content does not by itself make a psychological state capable of guiding
action *in the way a belief does*. If a psychological state that is not a belief
nonetheless is capable of guiding action in this way, it is capable of doing
so in virtue of the fact that it represents its propositional content, or
relates that propositional content to the world, in the way (whatever
exactly that is) that belief does.[20] It is this complex feature of having
propositional content and representing it, or relating it to the world, in a
certain way that is what I have called the action-guiding feature of belief.

---

[20] These locutions, admittedly vague, are meant to capture what it is that belief and
the other so-called cognitive attitudes have in common and that distinguishes them from
desire and the other so-called conative attitudes. This is often referred to as a psychological state or attitude's 'direction of fit', but that term is of limited use as different
philosophers use it in very different ways.

This problem—that an appearance cannot guide action in the way a belief does simply in virtue of possessing propositional content—is related to the more general question of what it is for something merely to appear to one to be the case. If it merely appears to me that the walls are blue, I am in a psychological state with the content *that* the walls are blue. But, in addition to having this propositional content, does this psychological state involve representing the proposition 'The walls are blue', or relating it to the world, in the way that the belief that the walls are blue does? This question poses a dilemma for Sextus. For if he argues that it does not, then an appearance cannot guide action in the way that a belief does. Yet if Sextus argues that an appearance does represent its propositional content, or relate it to the world, in the way a belief does, then he must also say exactly what it is, over and above representing its propositional content, or relating it to the world, in a certain way that makes a psychological state a belief. So Sextus must make the following complex argument in order to offer a full reply to the *apraxia* argument. He must argue (i) that an appearance is a psychological state with the complex feature of having propositional content and representing that content, or relating it to the world, in the way that belief does; (ii) that it is not *this* feature of a psychological state that makes it a belief and that it is possible for a psychological state to have this feature without being a belief; and (iii) that this is so because some other feature is the belief-making feature of a belief.

If Sextus can provide an account of the difference between an appearance and a belief, then he is in a position to argue that action does not require belief about how things are and, by doing so, to answer the *apraxia* argument. But, as I hope is now clear, providing an account of this sort is no small task. Suppose, though, that Sextus performs this task. At this point it is important to recognize that in arguing against the claim that action requires belief about how things are, Sextus is arguing against the claim that anyone who lacks beliefs of this kind must for that reason be *completely inactive* (ἀνενέργητος παντάπασιν).[21] The version of the *apraxia* argument to which Sextus replies is one according to which the Sceptic's lack of beliefs is incompatible with activity or behaviour *of any kind*.[22] Anyone who divests himself of his beliefs about how things are, as the Sceptic claims to do, will thereby be reduced to a state of complete paralysis. This is the version of the

---

[21] *PH* 1.23–4, 1.226; *M* 7.30, 11.165.
[22] On this point see especially Vogt, *Skepsis und Lebenspraxis*, 129–32.

apraxia argument made famous by Hume's claim that in the absence of belief 'All discourse, all action would immediately cease; and men remain in *a total lethargy*, till the necessities of nature, unsatisfied, put an end to their miserable existence.'[23]

There is, however, another version of the *apraxia* argument. According to this version of the argument, the Sceptic's lack of beliefs about how things are is incompatible not with activity or behaviour of any kind but with *action* where action is contrasted with the *mere animal activity or behaviour* exhibited by non-rational animals.[24] This is the version of the *apraxia* argument advanced by the Stoics against the Academics and their recommendation to suspend judgement about everything.[25] The Stoics did not argue that activity or behaviour of any kind requires belief and that, consequently, anyone who suspended judgement about everything would be reduced to complete inactivity. This was not a view the Stoics held. The Stoics did not deny that non-rational animals engage in various types of activity—including complex, goal-directed activity. However, they did deny that non-rational animals are able to assent to their impressions and form beliefs.[26] The Stoic view is that the kind of activity that constitutes action rather than mere animal activity, and so the kind of activity in virtue of which its subject is a morally responsible agent, requires belief and so the acts of assent through which beliefs are formed. The Stoics argued that anyone who follows the Academic recommendation, suspends judgement about everything, and so does not have any beliefs is incapable of this kind of activity.[27]

---

[23] Hume, *An Enquiry Concerning Human Understanding*, 12.23 (italics added).

[24] Cf. Striker, 'Sceptical Strategies', 102 and 108–9.

[25] Cicero, *Acad.* 1.45 attributes to Arcesilaus the claim that one should not assent to anything and so should suspend judgement about everything. D.L. 4.32, Plutarch, *Against Colotes* 1120C, and Sextus Empiricus, *PH* 1.232 report that Arcesilaus did, or at least claimed to, suspend judgement about everything.

[26] For the claim that the Stoics deny that animals assent to their impressions, see Sorabji, *Animal Minds & Human Morals*, 41, and Frede, 'The Stoic Conception of Reason', 51. I myself am not so sure that the texts Sorabji cites (Frede does not cite any text)—Clement, *Stromateis* 2.20, 110–11 (= SVF 2.714) and Origen, *On Principles* 3.1.3—support attributing to the Stoics the claim that non-rational animals lack assent rather than the weaker claim that non-rational animals lack a species of assent, namely, rational assent. But this complication does not matter for my purposes here. For even if the Stoics thought that non-rational animals lack only rational assent, it is this form of assent that they see the Academics as recommending one withhold universally and it is this form of assent that they take to be required for action rather than mere behaviour.

[27] See Origen, *On Principles* 3.1.2–3 (= LS 53A4–5) for the Stoic contrast between action or the movement of rational animals and mere animal behaviour or the movement of non-rational animals. This contrast depends, in turn, on the Stoic distinction between rational and non-rational impulse (ὁρμή). See Stobaeus 2.86–7 (= LS 53Q). For discussion of these matters, see Inwood, *Ethics and Human Action in Early Stoicism*, 66–91.

The Stoic version of the *apraxia* argument takes as its starting point the Stoic theory of action. That theory places a certain condition on an animal's activity being an action. That condition is, very roughly, that the activity be caused by the assent its subject gives to an impression with a certain kind of content.[28] The Stoics analyse action as activity that is caused by assent because they are concerned to show that freedom, and so moral responsibility, is compatible with determinism and they take assent to be the locus of free agency.[29] The important point for my purposes, however, is that a version of the *apraxia* argument that challenges not the existence but the status of the Sceptic's activities can take as its starting point *any* theory of action. So, for example, an argument against Scepticism that concedes the possibility of the Sceptic's being active but maintains that the Sceptic's activities are mere activities that fall short of action might take as its starting point the now standard account of action as an activity one engages in *for a reason*. And, on this account, doing something for a reason is in the paradigm case a matter of one's activity being motivated, and therefore caused, in the right way (whatever that is) by a combination of a *belief*—a belief about how things are—and a desire. Call this *the belief-desire model of action*.[30] Yet if belief about how things are is required for doing something for a reason, and the Sceptic divests himself of all beliefs of this kind, then the Sceptic is not capable of doing something for a reason. Hence, though he is active, and however complex his activities might be, these activities do not rise to the level of actions.[31] Yet (the argument concludes) whatever a human life is or ought to be, it is or ought to be a life of action, that is, a life that has as one of its features a distinctive kind of agency. I want to consider whether Sextus can

[28] The formulation of this condition is very rough because, of course, the details of the Stoic theory of action are more complicated. On that theory action is behaviour that is caused by a rational impulse. See Simplicius, *On Aristotle's Categories* (= SVF 2.499) for the definition of action as movement from a rational impulse (ἀπὸ λογικῆς ὁρμῆς). A rational impulse, in turn, is said either to be caused by or to be identical with assent given to an impression with a certain kind of content. (For the latter claim see Stobaeus 2.88.2–6 (= LS 33I), Galen, *On Hippocrates' and Plato's Doctrines* 4.3.7.) For discussion see, again, Inwood, *Ethics and Human Action in Early Stoicism*, 47–52.

[29] See Inwood, *Ethics and Human Action in Early Stoicism*, 66–72, and Bobzien, *Determinism and Freedom in Stoic Philosophy*, 239–42.

[30] See especially Davidson, 'Actions, Reasons, and Causes', 6, and Velleman, *The Possibility of Practical Reason*, 5–7 (who, however, rejects that identification of doing something for a reason with being motivated in the right way by a belief-desire combination).

[31] Cf. McPherran, 'Skeptical Homeopathy and Self-Refutation', 313.

respond to this version of the *apraxia* argument, and in doing so I am again concerned less with exegesis and more with those possibilities that fall within the logical space of Scepticism as Sextus describes it.

Here some will object that these logical possibilities are of no concern to Sextus. For why, they will ask, should Sextus have any interest in whether the Sceptic's activities satisfy those conditions that the belief-desire model, or any other philosophical theory of agency, places on action? Sextus needs only to argue that Scepticism is a possible way of life, and to do this he needs only to argue that the Sceptic can engage in the kind of complex, goal-directed activity that is required for living a life. Sextus, or the Sceptic he describes, suspends judgement about the soundness of any philosophical theory of agency and, indeed, about whether there is any distinction to be drawn between action and mere activity. All of this seems correct to me. But even if Sextus has no interest in the status of the Sceptic's activities given the belief-desire model (or any other philosophical theory of agency), *we* might, as *I* do, have such an interest—especially if we find, as I do, the belief-desire model of action plausible. One of the things we can do when we study the history of philosophy is to examine, in various ways, the philosophical resources of the view or theory or proposed way of life under discussion. We can consider whether, and how, this view or theory or proposed way of life can respond to the questions, or address the issues, or accommodate the concerns that *we*, with our own probably ineliminable philosophical preoccupations, bring to it. Of course, I do not say that this is the only thing we can do when we study the history of philosophy, or that it is something that anyone who studies the history of philosophy ought to do. But it is what I propose to do in the remainder of this chapter.

Sextus can grant for the sake of argument that action, as opposed to mere activity, is the doing of something for a reason. He must argue that doing something for a reason, and so acting rather than merely being active, does *not* require beliefs. But to see whether and how Sextus can make *this* argument we need to answer the following question. What contribution, on the belief-desire model of action, does the relevant belief make to the status of an activity as an action? Why, that is, does action, where action is contrasted with mere activity, require belief? Needless to say this is not a question that has preoccupied recent work in the philosophy of action.

According to the belief-desire model an activity is the doing of something for a reason, and hence an action, if and only if that activity has a certain kind of *cause*, namely, one that *rationalizes* it. A cause of this kind rationalizes the activity it causes in the sense that it explains what it is that makes the activity something the person engaged in it desires. Suppose I am engaged in some activity. On the belief-desire model the cause of my engagement in that activity explains what it is that makes the activity something I desire to do *only if* the cause of my engagement in that activity consists, in part, in a belief I have about the relation the activity bears to the satisfaction of some desire I have. This is my belief that the activity in question is the means to doing, or that it constitutes doing, something else I desire to do. So, for example, my raising my hand at a faculty meeting is something I do for a reason, and hence an action, if and only if it has a cause that rationalizes it in the sense I have described. This cause explains what it is that makes raising my hand something I desire to do. And it can do so only if it consists, in part, in a belief I have about the relation the activity of raising my hand bears to the satisfaction of some desire I have. This will be my belief that raising my hand is the means to doing something else I desire to do (catch the attention of the chair, speak on the matter under discussion) or constitutes doing something I desire to do (vote on a motion, stretch my arm). On the belief-desire model, then, action requires belief because action requires that an agent have some belief about the relation her behaviour bears to the satisfaction of a desire she has, namely, the belief that her behaviour satisfies, or at least promotes the satisfaction of, her desire. If I do not believe that raising my arm satisfies or promotes the satisfaction of some desire I have, then there is nothing that explains what it is that makes raising my arm something I desire to do. *A fortiori* the cause of my raising my arm does not explain what it is that makes raising my arm something I desire to do. Hence, the cause of my raising my arm does not rationalize my raising my arm; and if this is so, then on the belief-desire model my raising my arm is not an action. The desire that motivates, and hence causes, an activity cannot by itself rationalize that activity. My desire to raise my arm cannot by itself explain what makes the bodily movement that is in fact a raising of my arm something I desire to do. Given my desire to raise my arm it remains unexplained why I make *this* bodily movement to satisfy that desire. The belief-desire model of action claims that the only thing that can explain this is my belief that the bodily movement constitutes raising my arm and so satisfies the desire I have to raise my arm.

It is not difficult to see what sort of response Sextus can offer to this line of thought. He can grant that an activity is the doing of something for a reason, and hence an action, only if the cause of that activity rationalizes it. Sextus can argue, however, that it is *not* the case that the cause of an activity rationalizes it only if that cause consists, in part, of a *belief* about the relation that activity bears to the satisfaction of a desire one has. An appearance can play the same role in causing *and* rationalizing an activity that, on the belief-desire model of action, a belief does. The Sceptic raises his arm because he has a certain desire and it appears to him, though he does not believe, that raising his arm satisfies that desire. The appearance that in conjunction with a desire causes the Sceptic to raise his arm—the appearance that raising his arm satisfies the desire—explains what it is about raising his arm that makes it something the Sceptic desires to do. If this is so, then the Sceptic's raising his arm has as its cause the combination of an appearance and a desire, and this cause rationalizes it. It follows that, at least according to the belief-desire model of action, raising his arm is something the Sceptic does for a reason and so is an action rather than a mere activity.

The claim that an appearance can play the same role in causing and rationalizing an activity that, on the belief-desire model, a belief does can be understood in the following way. The Sceptic raises his arm because it appears to him that doing so satisfies a desire he has. Its appearing to the Sceptic that raising his arm satisfies a desire he has is, at least in the context of the activity of raising his arm, a matter of the Sceptic's not believing but nonetheless treating it as true that raising his arm satisfies a desire he has. There is nothing mysterious about treating as true a proposition one does not believe to be true, and we do so when, for example, we assume something for the sake of argument, form a hypothesis, or engage in imaginative play with a child. Action, understood as an activity whose cause rationalizes it, requires not that an agent *believe*, but only that she *treat it as true*, that her activity satisfies a desire she has.[32] *This* claim, at least, has some plausibility. It is plausible to think that action can be the product of a desire in conjunction with an attitude that falls short of belief

---

[32] Cf. Striker, 'Sceptical Strategies', 112. Striker introduces a distinction, which she attributes to Carneades, between 'accepting as true' and 'adopting as a basis for action'. This distinction, she claims, is the background for the Sceptic's distinction between criteria of truth and criteria of action. The point of the distinction between these two kinds of criteria, she writes, is that the Sceptic 'acts in accordance with what appears to him to be the case without committing himself to the truth of his impressions'. Striker does not explain what it might mean for the Sceptic to act in this way. Her view seems to be that if it appears to the Sceptic that p, for the relevant range of values for p, then the Sceptic acts on the basis of p, or adopts p as a basis for action, without accepting p as true. But talk of acting on the basis of a p or adopting p as a basis for action is intelligible only if it is understood to mean that the Sceptic treats p as true without believing p.

but nonetheless involves treating its propositional content as true. Suppose that I become lost while driving and want to get back to the highway. I come to an intersection and, being lost, have no beliefs about how to get back to the highway from where I am now. So if I turn left I do so *without* believing that by turning left I will get to the highway. But I turn left rather than turning right or continuing straight through the intersection because I treat it as true—by, for instance, assuming or hypothesizing—that by turning left I will get to the highway.

This response to the second version of the *apraxia* argument invites at least the following two objections. First, suppose that it is possible for me to treat a certain proposition *p* as true without believing *p*, and that it is possible for me to perform an action *because*, though I do not believe *p*, I treat *p* as true. Nonetheless my doing so depends upon my having a substantial body of beliefs about the world. If that is so, then action, as opposed to mere activity, still requires beliefs even if it is not the case that in order for an activity to be an action it must have as one of its causes the belief that the activity satisfies a desire one has. To answer this objection Sextus must argue that it is not necessary for the Sceptic to have some beliefs in order to treat certain propositions as true in the context of his activities. But if in the context of activity treating *p* as true is, or is part of, what it is for it to appear to one that *p*, then Sextus must argue that it is possible to have appearances without having any beliefs.

Second, even if it is possible to have appearances without having beliefs, and even if at least in certain contexts having an appearance involves treating its propositional content as true, it does not follow that an appearance has the same motivational force, and so the same capacity to rationalize action, that belief does. This is so because it is not the case that *any* attitude that falls short of belief but involves treating its propositional content as true can, in conjunction with a desire, motivate action. In imagining that there is food in the refrigerator, I treat it as true that there is food in the refrigerator. But if I am hungry—that is, if I am really hungry and not just imagining that I am hungry—and I merely imagine that there is food in the refrigerator, I will not be motivated to go and open it.[33] The second objection is simply that for all Sextus has

---

[33] This is most obviously the case if I know or believe that there is no food in the refrigerator. The claim here is not that imagination can't motivate action, but that it can't do so in conjunction with desire. So if in imaginative play imagination does motivate us to act, it does so in combination with some 'mock-desire', that is, some conative attitude that is not a desire but an analogue to desire in the way imagination is an analogue to belief. On these issues see Velleman, 'On the Aim of Belief', especially 256–63 and 269–73.

said it is possible that even if an appearance is an attitude that involves treating its propositional content as true, it is one that, unlike belief, fails to motivate action. Thus Sextus must argue that an appearance involves treating its propositional content as true in just the way belief, and the other attitudes that have the same motivational force as belief, do. It should be clear that whether and how Sextus can make this argument, and the argument he must make to respond to the first objection, depends on whether he can given an adequate account of what an appearance is and how it differs from a belief.

It is a striking feature of the Sceptic's psychology that he does not endorse any desire he has. According to Sextus, the Sceptic does not believe about anything either that it is good or that it is bad. Therefore, he does not believe about anything he desires either that it is good or that it is bad. If the Sceptic desires x but does not believe that x is good, this is so because it appears to him that he has no reason to believe that x is good. But its appearing to the Sceptic that he has no reason to believe that x is *good* is no different from its appearing to him that he has no reason to believe that x is *desirable* in the sense of *being worth desiring*. And if this is how things appear to the Sceptic, it appears to him that even though he desires x, he has no reason to believe that there is some consideration that counts in favour of or justifies desiring x. Hence, it appears to the Sceptic that he has no reason to believe that *in this sense* there is a reason for him to desire x. The Sceptic fails to endorse any desire he has insofar as he fails to believe about anything he desires that it is good, and so worth desiring, and that he has a reason to desire it.

It is important to be clear that it does *not* follow from the fact that the Sceptic fails to endorse any desire he has that, for anything he desires, it appears to the Sceptic that he has no reason to desire it. It is important, in other words, to distinguish these two appearances:

(1) It appears to me that I have no reason to believe there is a reason for me to desire x.

(2) It appears to me that there is no reason for me to desire x.

The Sceptic who desires x is subject to appearance (1), and that is why he suspends judgement about whether there is a reason for him to desire x where that is a matter of suspending judgement about whether x is good in the sense of being worth desiring. But the Sceptic who desires x need not be subject to appearance (2). If the Sceptic desires x, it is possible, even likely, that although he fails to *believe* that x is good in the sense of being worth desiring, it *appears* to him that *x* is good in this sense. Yet if it appears to the Sceptic that *x* is good in the sense of being worth desiring, then it appears to the Sceptic that there is a reason for him to desire *x*. The Sceptic's arguments undermine the status of any consideration to be a reason to believe that *x* is good. As a result it appears to the Sceptic that there is no reason to believe that *x* is good. However, these arguments leave intact the appearance the Sceptic has that *x* is good. The Sceptic is now in the position in which it appears to him that there is no reason to believe that things are as they appear to him to be. Yet it still appears to the Sceptic that *x* is good in the sense of being worth desiring. And the notion of there being a reason for one to desire *x* is embedded in the notion of *x*'s being good in the sense of worth desiring. If the Sceptic's arguments leave intact the appearance that *x* is good in the sense of being worth desiring, they also leave intact the appearance that there is a reason for one to desire *x*.

So the Sceptic who desires *x* can be, and presumably often is, subject to the following two appearances:

(3) It appears to me that *x* is good and so worth desiring.
(4) It appears to me that I have no reason to believe that *x* is good and so worth desiring.

Insofar as the Sceptic is subject to appearances (3) and (4) he is also subject to these two appearances:

(5) It appears to me that there is a reason for me to desire *x*.
(6) It appears to me that I have no reason to believe that there is a reason for me to desire x.

If the Sceptic is subject to appearances (3) and (4) and (5) and (6), his being so is just an instance of the more general situation in which the Sceptic, in virtue of his Scepticism, invariably finds himself. So, for example, the Sceptic might be subject to the following two appearances:

(7) It appears to me that grass is green.
(8) It appears to me that I have no reason to believe that grass is green.

In being subject to the appearances (3) and (4) and (5) and (6), just as in being subject to the appearances (7) and (8), the Sceptic is in a situation in which it appears to him that *p* but, given what appears to him to be the force of his Sceptical arguments, it also appears to him that he has no reason to believe *p*.

It is a consequence of the Sceptic's failure to endorse any desire he has that the explanation the Sceptic can give of his own behaviour is similar in an important respect to the explanation the unwilling addict can give of his addictive behaviour. The unwilling addict can explain his addictive behaviour by appeal to an addictive desire he has, e.g. a desire for a drug to which he is addicted, and a belief about the means to its satisfaction. Insofar as the unwilling addict is an *addict*, he has a desire to take the drug to which he is addicted that is stronger than any desire he has not to take that drug. That, after all, is just part of what it is to be addicted to a drug. But someone is an *unwilling* rather than a *willing* addict insofar as he believes that taking the drug is bad, or at least worse than not taking it, and in addition to his stronger desire to take that drug has a weaker desire not to take it *and* a second-order desire that his desire to take the drug be weaker than his desire not to take it. This second-order desire is the desire that his first-order desire to take the drug not be the desire that moves him to act.[34] In this way the unwilling addict can explain his addictive behaviour by appeal to his addictive desire and the relevant belief while at the same time failing to believe that, all things considered, he has a reason to desire what he most desires or to do what he in fact does.

The unwilling addict fails to believe about the object of his addictive desire that it is something good, and he fails to do so because he believes that it is something bad. The Sceptic fails to believe about the object of *any* desire he has that it is something good, and he fails to do so because he suspends judgement about whether anything is good or bad. If we draw a distinction between *desiring* something and *valuing* it, where to value something is not only to desire it but also to believe it to be good, then just as the unwilling addict desires without valuing the drug to which he is addicted, so the Sceptic desires without valuing *anything* he in fact desires.[35]

---

[34] See especially Frankfurt, 'Freedom of the Will and the Concept of a Person', 17–18.

[35] The distinction between desiring something and valuing it is drawn differently by different philosophers. See, for example, Watson, 'Free Agency', 340–8, and Smith, *The Moral Problem*, 133–6. This conception of valuing something—one according to which to value something requires that one believe it to be good—might appear overly restrictive. For, the thought is, the Sceptic can value something simply by having a preference for it and even if this preference is not underwritten by the belief, which the Sceptic lacks, that its object is something good. (Thanks to Richard Bett for suggesting this possibility to me.) But it is difficult to see how the Sceptic's preferences are anything different from, or more than, his desires. The Sceptic might have a preference for the wines of Burgundy, or he might prefer them to the wines of Bordeaux, but this is just a matter of the Sceptic's having a desire for wines of the first type, or a desire for wines of the first type that is stronger than any desire he has for wines of the second type. For the

The unwilling addict not only fails to value what he (most strongly) desires, but he values *something else*—the object of a weaker desire he has. In this way the unwilling addict experiences a conflict between what he values and what he (most strongly) desires. The Sceptic, in contrast, does not experience any conflict of this sort. For the Sceptic does not value anything if to value something is, in part, to believe it to be good. But a conflict between what one values and what one (most strongly) desires is not necessary, even if it is sufficient, for a failure to endorse a desire one has. All that is required in order for a person to fail to endorse a desire she has is that she fail to value the object of that desire. This failure, however, does not require that there is something else—the object of some other and weaker desire she has—she does value. One way in which a person can fail to value what she desires, and the way in which the Sceptic does so, is by failing to value anything at all.[36]

If the Sceptic does not endorse any desire he has, then he will explain *all* of his behaviour in just the way the unwilling addict explains his addictive behaviour. But in explaining his addictive behaviour the unwilling addict adopts the following kind of third-person stance toward it. He explains his addictive behaviour by attributing to the subject of that behaviour a desire for something he himself does not value. And that is the way in which one person can (and, of course, often does) explain the behaviour of another person. So, for example, I explain Jones's addictive behaviour by attributing to him as his strongest desire a desire for the drug to which he is addicted. But I myself do not believe that the object of the desire I attribute to Jones is something good in the sense of being worth desiring. Hence, I attribute to Jones a desire for something I myself do not value. So, on the one hand, I explain Jones's addictive behaviour by appeal to a cause—his desire for the drug together with the relevant belief—that rationalizes that behaviour. On the other hand, since I do not value what

Sceptic to prefer something just is for him to desire it, or desire it more than he desires something else, and the point is that there is nothing that the Sceptic prefers or desires that he also values. And this is so because there is *nothing* the Sceptic values in the sense that he believes it to be good.

[36] Though the Sceptic does not experience any conflict between what he values and what he (most strongly) desires, it is possible for him to experience a conflict between what appears to him to be good and what he (most strongly) desires. Nothing Sextus says indicates that according to him the Sceptic desires all and only those things that appear to him to be good in the sense of being worth desiring. But whether and how conflict of the first sort is different from conflict of the second sort will depend on whether and how belief is different from appearance.

I take Jones to desire, I do not believe that there is some consideration that counts in favour of or justifies Jones's addictive desire or the behaviour it causes. In this sense, and despite the fact that I can explain Jones's addictive behaviour in a way that rationalizes it, I do not believe that there is a reason for Jones to behave as he does. The stance I adopt toward Jones's addictive behaviour—that is, the stance I adopt toward *someone else's* addictive behaviour—is just the stance the unwilling addict adopts toward his own addictive behaviour. It is also, and this is the important point, the stance the Sceptic adopts toward *all* of his behaviour. The Sceptic can explain his own behaviour by appeal to a cause—a desire he has together with the relevant appearance—that rationalizes that behaviour. Yet the Sceptic does not value anything he desires, and his failure to do so means that he does not believe that there is some consideration that counts in favour of or justifies his desire or the behaviour it causes. In *this* sense the Sceptic, in virtue of his Scepticism, does not believe that there is a reason for him to behave as he does.

This fact, however, has no bearing on the question whether, as far as the belief-desire model of action goes, the Sceptic's behaviour is mere activity rather than action. Action is supposed to be the doing of something for a reason. But doing something for a reason, in the sense in which it is supposed to be constitutive of action on the belief-desire model, does *not* require that a person believe that there is some consideration that counts in favour of or justifies her behaviour and that, in this sense, there is a reason for her to behave as she does.[37] For, otherwise, the unwilling addict's behaviour, and other types of irrational or perverse behaviour, would fail to count as action. Yet, at least on the belief-desire model of action, these types of behaviour do count as (a species of) action. I have suggested that Sextus can claim that the Sceptic's behaviour has a cause—desire he has together with the relevant appearance—that rationalizes it. The plausibility of this claim, as of other claims Sextus makes about Scepticism, depends on whether and how an appearance as Sextus understands it is different from a belief. But if this claim is plausible, then it is plausible to think that in the sense

---

[37] Unless, that is, the belief-desire model of action conceives of desires as value judgements—as, for instance, Davidson sometimes seems to do. See 'Intending', 102 where he claims that 'wanting and desiring are best viewed as corresponding to, or constituting, prima facie judgements'; and 'How is Weakness of the Will Possible?', 31 where he claims that 'when a person acts with an intention . . . he sets a positive value on some state of affairs'. But contrast 'Actions, Reasons, and Causes', 4 where Davidson denies that desires or other pro-attitudes are 'convictions . . . that every action of a certain kind ought to be performed, is worth performing, or is, all things considered, desirable.'

relevant to the belief-desire model of action, the Sceptic's behaviour is the doing of something for a reason and, therefore, an action rather than a mere activity. If this is so, then the version of the *apraxia* argument that challenges not the existence but the status of the Sceptic's activity, and does so on the basis of the belief-desire model of action, fails.[38]

The belief-desire model of action is not, of course, the only possible, or even the most persuasive, account of what an action is. Some philosophers have drawn a distinction between action and motivated activity. Motivated activity is understood as behaviour that is caused in the right way (whatever that is) by attitudes that rationalize it. So understood motivated activity is different from mere bodily movement. An account of action that accepts the distinction between action and motivated activity claims that action—or what is sometimes called 'autonomous' or 'full-blooded' action—requires something more than motivated activity.[39] It is clear, I think, that the more demanding an account of action is, the less plausible it is that the Sceptic's behaviour— or, for that matter, the behaviour of most of us non-Sceptics most of the time—qualifies as action. But the point relevant to my present concerns is the following. The version of the *apraxia* argument that challenges the status of the Sceptic's behaviour will take as its basis an account of what action is. The more demanding this account of action is, the less effective it is as a basis for this version of the *apraxia* argument against Scepticism. For Sextus can argue, first, that one or more conditions this account places on action are not in fact conditions on action but, at most, conditions on one type of action; and, second, that it is not a strike against Scepticism that it renders the Sceptic incapable of action of this type.

---

[38] This will be so even if we supplement the belief-desire model of action with intentions. The formation and execution of intentions is standardly thought to be essential to action. Yet on one view an intention involves, or perhaps just is, a belief: if I intend to ϕ, then I believe I will ϕ. (See, for instance, Harman, 'Practical Reasoning', 150–3, and Velleman, 'Practical Reflection', 51–4.) If the Sceptic has no beliefs about how things are, and so no beliefs about how things will be, he does not have intentions; and if he lacks intentions, then though he can be active, he cannot act. It should be clear that Sextus can claim that any belief requirement on intention can be satisfied by appearances as well: if the non-Sceptic's intentions are, or involve, beliefs, the Sceptic's intentions are, or involve, appearances. It should be no less clear that the plausibility of this claim turns, as so much else does, on whether and how an appearance as Sextus understands it is different from a belief.

[39] See, for example, the so-called 'hierarchical model' of action introduced by Frankfurt in 'Freedom of the Will and the Concept of a Person' and other papers; and the even more demanding account of action presented by Velleman in *The Possibility of Practical Reason*, esp. 14–31.

It is, however, difficult to resist the thought that there is something problematic about the stance the Sceptic adopts toward his desires and the behaviour they cause. The Sceptic does not believe that there is a reason for him to desire anything he does desire. As a result, he does not believe that there is a reason for him to behave in any way he does behave. In failing to endorse any desire he has the Sceptic fails to endorse any behaviour his desires motivate and so cause. And in failing to endorse his own behaviour the Sceptic stands at a distance from that behaviour: he regards it in one of the ways in which one person regards the behaviour of another person. To this extent, at least, the Sceptic does not regard his behaviour as *his* behaviour.[40] That this is so raises the question whether or how or to what extent the Sceptic *participates* in his own behaviour. It is not easy to understand the kind of participation in one's behaviour that, some philosophers have claimed, is required for at least the distinctively human form of agency. But it is also not easy to dismiss the thought that there is a distinctively human form of agency and that it does require the agent to participate in her behaviour in a way the Sceptic fails to do. Sextus here faces something close to a dilemma. He will insist that it does or at least can appear to the Sceptic, even if the Sceptic does not believe, that there is a reason for him to desire what he desires and to do what he does. Yet if its so appearing to the Sceptic constitutes a genuine endorsement of his own desires and behaviour, then, once again, it is not easy to see how an appearance is different from a belief. Yet if an appearance is different from a belief, as Sextus must say it is, then it is not easy to see how its appearing to the Sceptic that there is a reason for him to desire what he desires and to do what he does can constitute a genuine endorsement of his own desires and behaviour. Endorsement of the sort some philosophers have thought to be distinctive of human agency requires no more and no less than belief.

---

[40] The Sceptic's failure to endorse his behaviour, and the kind of third-person stance he thereby adopts toward it, is very different from the detachment from oneself that Burnyeat, 'Can the Sceptic Live his Scepticism?', 56–7, attributes to the Sceptic. For Burnyeat the Sceptic is detached from himself to the extent that he is detached from the assent that, he argues, he must give to certain appearances he has—namely, those appearances whose content is a 'philosophical' proposition. For, Burnyeat claims, if *p* is a 'philosophical' as opposed to perceptual proposition, then its appearing to me that *p* just is my assenting to, and so believing, that *p*. Burnyeat provides no argument for this claim, and, as Johnsen 'On the Coherence of Pyrrhonian Skepticism', 547–8, has made clear, it is dubious at best.

Sextus must argue that if the Sceptic fails to exhibit the distinctively human form of agency, that is so because participation in one's own behaviour, and the form of agency that requires it, are, as it appears to the Sceptic, obstacles to tranquillity. For they require that we value something—that is, that we believe about something that it is good—and that we desire, or desire most strongly, what we value. But, Sextus argues, the value we attach to what we desire and the efforts we make to direct our desires toward what we value are sources of distress and anxiety. The Sceptic is like anyone else a bodily creature, and as such he cannot avoid this distress and anxiety by divesting himself of his desires. But he can cease to value what he desires, and so abandon any effort to direct his desires toward what he values, by divesting himself of his beliefs.

Scepticism, as Sextus describes it, is supposed to remove from one's life those distinctively human obstacles to tranquillity. The problem—and this, it seems to me, is the fundamental problem with Scepticism—is that it can do so only by removing from one's life some of its distinctively, and most important, human features. Scepticism purports to make us more tranquil by making us less human. The question is how much less human Scepticism makes us and whether, as Sextus presents the matter, a tranquil life can be a recognizably human one at all.

Conclusion

Scepticism as Sextus presents it in the *Outlines of Pyrrhonism* is sometimes characterized by commentators as a form of anti-rationalism. The
Sceptic is said to be an anti-rationalist insofar as he renounces reason as
a guide to life, and the Sceptic is said to do this insofar as he abandons
the search for truth and gives up any attempt to resolve by argument or
reasoning conflicts between candidates for belief. On this line of
thought the Sceptic's anti-rationalism has one of two possible motives.
Sextus insists repeatedly that the Sceptic is not committed to the view
that knowledge or reasonable belief is impossible. But, it is claimed, the
Sceptic's arguments—specifically, the Agrippan modes—commit him
to this view. If the Sceptic is a negative dogmatist, then he abandons the
search for truth on the grounds that it cannot succeed.[1] Alternatively,
the Sceptic's anti-rationalism is motivated by a view about the conditions of tranquillity (ἀταραξία). The Sceptic takes tranquillity as his
ultimate end or goal. He abandons the search for truth on the grounds
that even if it is successful, it cannot lead to tranquillity: it appears to the
Sceptic that tranquillity can be achieved *only* through suspension of
judgement.[2] So the Sceptic seeks suspension of judgement rather than
truth, and to the extent he achieves it he lives a life guided by appearances rather than reason.

It seems to me that the interpretation of Scepticism as a form of anti-
rationalism fails to capture what is most central to Scepticism as Sextus
describes it in the *Outlines of Pyrrhonism*. Sextus denies that the Sceptic

---

[1] See especially Striker, 'Scepticism as a Kind of Philosophy', 120–1. Striker thinks
that in its negative dogmatism, and so its anti-rationalism, Scepticism resembles the early
Empirical school of medicine. On the relation of early Empiricism to Scepticism, see
especially Frede, 'The Ancient Empiricists', 248–9.

[2] Striker, 'Scepticism as a Kind of Philosophy', 122, claims that part of the rationale
for the Sceptic's anti-rationalism is 'that abandoning the search for truth will give you
peace of mind'. See also Cooper, 'Arcesilaus: Socratic and Sceptic', 101, who writes that
for the Sceptic getting rid of the ideal of reason as a guide to life 'is the essential—both
necessary and sufficient—condition for living an unperturbed life'.

is a negative dogmatist, and this denial is suspect only if the Sceptic's use of the Agrippan modes commits him to the view that knowledge or reasonable belief is impossible. But, as I argued in Chapter 1, it does so only if the Sceptic is also, and independently of his use of the Agrippan modes, committed to the view that there are not and cannot be what I have called *basic reasons*, that is, self-evident truths that can be used to establish the truth of candidates for belief whose truth is not self-evident. And, I claimed, none of the Sceptic's arguments commits him to *that* view. The Sceptic is a negative dogmatist about knowledge or reasonable belief only if he is also, and independently of his negative dogmatism about knowledge or reasonable belief, a negative dogmatist about basic reasons. Since the Sceptic is not a negative dogmatist of the latter sort, he is not a negative dogmatist of the former sort. Since that is so, the Sceptic does not abandon the search for truth on the grounds that it cannot succeed.

Nor does the Sceptic abandon the search for truth on the grounds that he cannot achieve his ultimate aim, tranquillity, by engaging in it. First, the Sceptic does not *in general* subscribe to the view that suspension of judgement is the necessary means to tranquillity. The qualifier 'in general' is required here in view of Sextus' use at *PH* 1.27–8 of what I have called *the value argument*. This argument, I will claim below, is an expression of a deviant, because clearly anti-rationalist, strand in Scepticism. Second, as I argued in Chapter 1, the account Sextus gives of the Sceptic's motivation for seeking tranquillity is coherent only if the Sceptic has an interest in the discovery of truth for its own sake and not merely as a means to tranquillity. For the Sceptic seeks tranquillity insofar as he seeks relief from the distress he experiences as a result of not knowing which of two or more conflicting candidates for belief is true. This distress is intelligible only if the Sceptic has an interest in truth—an interest, that is, in knowing which of two conflicting candidates for belief is true—and this cannot be an interest in truth *as* a means to tranquillity. For any interest the Sceptic has in truth as a means to tranquillity presupposes, and so cannot explain, the distress the Sceptic experiences. The Sceptic is interested in truth as a means to tranquillity only if he is *already* distressed by a conflict between candidates for belief and it appears to him that he can relieve his distress, and so achieve a measure of tranquillity, by discovering which of the conflicting candidates for belief is true. So the Sceptic must have an interest in truth that precedes, and explains, the distress he experiences, and this must be an interest in truth that does not depend on any connection the discovery of truth might appear to have to tranquillity. In this sense, or to this extent, it must be an interest in truth for its own sake. But if the Sceptic does not deny the possibility of achieving tranquillity by discovering the truth, and if he has an interest in the discovery of truth for its own sake, then what he has most reason to do is to pursue his ultimate aim, tranquillity, by means of the search for truth. This is so even if, as it is plausible to think, it appears to the Sceptic that tranquillity can be achieved through suspension of judgement. For the Sceptic's interest in truth for its own sake gives him a reason to take the discovery of truth rather than suspension of judgement as the means to achieving tranquillity.

There is an additional problem with the interpretation of Scepticism as a form of anti-rationalism. The claim that the Sceptic discards reason as a guide to thought and action is difficult to reconcile with the way in which, according to Sextus, the Sceptic suspends judgement. For the Sceptic suspends judgement about whether p when and only when, as it appears to him, he has no reason to believe either p or its negation—that is, when and only when, as it appears to him, no consideration he is aware of favours the truth of p over its negation, or vice versa. If the Sceptic is an anti-rationalist, however, then it is just a coincidence that he suspends judgement when and only when, as it appears to him, reason requires him to do so. Moreover, it is not just that the Sceptic suspends judgement when and only when, as it happens, reason requires him to do so, but that he suspends judgement *in full recognition* that reason requires him to do so. As a result, the interpretation of Scepticism as a form of anti-rationalism must claim that though the Sceptic suspends judgement in full recognition that reason requires him to do so, the Sceptic does not suspend judgement *because* he recognizes that reason requires him to do so.[3]

It is important to be clear about how this claim is to be understood. The interpretation of Scepticism as a form of anti-rationalism does not deny that its appearing to the Sceptic that he has no reason to believe either p or its negation *causes* the Sceptic to suspend judgement about whether p. In fact, this causal connection will be said to explain the sense in which, according to Sextus, if it appears to the Sceptic that he has no

---

[3] See Cooper, 'Arcesilaus: Socratic and Sceptic', 101–2 who writes that the (Pyrrhonian) Sceptic 'keeps on suspending each time, in recognition, to be sure, of the fact that critical reason, if it were to be followed, would demand this . . . But he does not suspend *because* reason, if followed fully and correctly, does demand this. His suspensions are not faithful, devoted acts of critical reason.'

reason to believe either *p* or its negation, it is *necessary* for him to suspend judgement about whether *p*. The claim that the Sceptic does not suspend judgement *because* he recognizes that reason requires him to do so is the claim that the Sceptic does not suspend judgement *in order to* do what, as it appears to him, reason requires him to do. *This* claim is not supported by Sextus' text. For, as I argued in Chapter 2, according to Sextus the Sceptic suspends judgement with the aim of satisfying what appears to him to be a rational requirement. If this is right, then the necessity that characterizes the Sceptic's suspension of judgement is in the first instance hypothetical: it is necessary for the Sceptic to suspend judgement if he is to satisfy, as he aims to do, what appears to him to be a requirement of reason. The Sceptic has the aim of satisfying what he takes to be the basic requirements of reason because part of what it is to be engaged in the search for truth, as according to Sextus the Sceptic is, is to have this aim. So in suspending judgement the Sceptic as Sextus describes him is guided by reason. If this is so, the Sceptic is not an anti-rationalist.

In denying, as I am, that Scepticism is a form of anti-rationalism, I do not mean to deny that reason plays a restricted role in the life, and especially the action, of the Sceptic. I mean to deny only that the restricted role reason plays in the Sceptic's life constitutes a form of anti-rationalism. The Sceptic suspends judgement when he does be-cause, as it appears to him, reason requires him to do so. The Sceptic's suspension of judgement is, therefore, directly guided by reason. But, again as it appears to the Sceptic, reason requires him to suspend judgement about *everything* where that, as I argued in Chapter 3, is a matter of suspending judgement universally about how things are rather than merely appear to one to be. If the Sceptic has no beliefs about how things are, then reason fails to guide his thought and action in the sense that the Sceptic does not make inferences from his beliefs about how things are and by doing so form new beliefs about how things are or about what he will or ought to do. The Sceptic restricts the role of reason in his life by divesting himself of the beliefs on which reason operates.[4] So the fact that reason plays a restricted role in the Sceptic's life is a consequence of the fact that the Sceptic has no beliefs about how things are. But the fact that the Sceptic has no beliefs about how things are is a consequence of the Sceptic's efforts to satisfy what appear to him to be the requirements of reason. In this way the restriction placed on

---

[4] Cf. Johnsen, 'On the Coherence of Pyrrhonian Skepticism', 528.

the role of reason in the Sceptic's life is a restriction reason places on itself. If this is so, then it is a mistake to view the Sceptic's policy of following appearances as a renunciation of reason as a guide to thought and action. For in following appearances the Sceptic is indirectly following reason: reason requires the Sceptic to follow appearances insofar as it requires him to live without beliefs.

In arguing that the Sceptic is not an anti-rationalist I have given little attention to one aspect of Scepticism. This is Scepticism as a therapeutic practice. The therapeutic strand in Scepticism seems to me to have little connection with the other features of Scepticism as Sextus describes it in *Outlines of Pyrrhonism*.[5] Nonetheless, it is clearly on display in the closing paragraphs of that work where Sextus tells us that the Sceptic is philanthropic (φιλάνθρωπος) and 'wishes to cure by argument, as far as possible, the conceit and rashness of the dogmatists (τὴν τῶν δογματικῶν οἴησίν τε καὶ προπέτειαν κατὰ δύναμιν ἰᾶσθαι λόγῳ βούλεται)' (*PH* 3.280).[6] This fact is supposed to explain why the Sceptic's arguments sometimes are, and even appear to the Sceptic himself to be, weak. For, according to Sextus, a weak argument is sometimes sufficient to induce suspension of judgement in a person whose dogmatism the Sceptic wants to cure.[7]

The conception of Scepticism as therapy is evident especially in Sextus' use of *the value argument*. According to that argument belief of a certain kind—the belief about something either that it is good or that it is bad—is pathogenic.[8] For *any* belief of this kind, true or false,

---

[5] Here I disagree with, for example, Annas, *The Morality of Happiness*, 246.

[6] I suspect that the therapeutic strand of Scepticism finds expression in *PH* 1.18 as well. There Sextus denies that the Sceptic is engaged in philosophical investigation of the natural world (φυσιολογία). The Sceptic makes himself familiar with the views and claims on offer in this part of philosophy, but he does so only in order to be able to bring about suspension of judgement and, through suspension of judgement, tranquillity. Moreover, Sextus says that what is true of the Sceptic with respect to natural philosophy is also true with respect to the other major parts of philosophy (logic and ethics). So, according to Sextus at *PH* 1.18, the Sceptic is not engaged in philosophy at all.

[7] Mates, *The Skeptic Way*, 314, suggests that *PH* 3.280–1 is an interpolation inserted into the text sometime between Sextus and our earliest manuscripts of *PH*. This suggestion is implausible, even wildly so, but, like Mates, I find little of philosophical interest or value in the therapeutic strand of Scepticism.

[8] Nussbaum, *The Therapy of Desire*, 284, generalizes without textual warrant what Sextus says about one kind of belief—belief about something's being either good or bad—to *all* belief. In this way she misleadingly presents what is in fact only one strand of Scepticism as Sextus describes it as the whole of Scepticism. She talks throughout her discussion as though Scepticism were simply something she calls 'Skeptical therapy' (see especially 285–6 where she describes the definition Sextus gives at *PH* 1.8 of Scepticism as a definition of Skeptical therapy). Nussbaum's illicit generalization of Sextus' claim about one kind of belief to all belief is the basis for her claims about the purgative nature of the Sceptic's arguments or use of reason.

warranted or not, is a source of distress and anxiety. The only way in which a person can rid himself of this distress and anxiety, and protect himself against its recurrence, is by ceasing to believe about anything either that it is good or that it is bad. The upshot of the value argument, then, is that there is a disease—one whose outbreak is in fact pandemic—for which the only treatment is suspension of judgement. If the value argument is supposed to provide us with reason to adopt Scepticism as a way of life, it does so by presenting Scepticism as a cure for what ails.

The conception of Scepticism as therapy might seem also to lie behind Sextus' comparison at *PH* 2.188 of the Sceptic's arguments to purgative drugs. For he writes there that the Sceptic's arguments against the existence of proof, 'like purgative drugs which evacuate themselves along with the matters present in the body, can actually cancel themselves along with the other arguments which are said to be probative'.[9] The implication of this comparison might seem to be that for the Sceptic arguments, like drugs, are simply therapeutic agents. In my view, however, to read the passage in this way is to misunderstand it. First, Sextus does not compare *all* of the Sceptic's arguments, but only the Sceptic's arguments against proof, to purgative drugs. Sextus says that the arguments that can cancel themselves like purgative drugs are those that *also* cancel any argument the dogmatic philosopher takes to be a proof. The only arguments the Sceptic has that do *this* are his arguments against the existence of proof. Second, the capacity of the Sceptic's arguments against proof to cancel themselves is *not* a capacity to bring about some psychological, and so therapeutic, effect in those who are exposed to these arguments. As Sextus describes it in this passage, an argument's cancelling itself is a strictly logical phenomenon: it is a matter of that argument establishing the truth of a conclusion whose truth, in turn, undermines the claim of the argument to have established it. In claiming that the Sceptic's arguments against proof cancel themselves Sextus is simply attempting to make a virtue out of a necessity. This claim is Sextus' response to the dogmatic philosopher's charge that any Sceptical argument against proof necessarily fails if it succeeds. The dogmatic philosopher insists that any argument that

---

[9] Annas and Barnes, *Outlines*, translate οἱ λόγοι in the first sentence of *PH* 2.188 as 'Arguments'. By failing to translate the definite article they make Sextus' claim in this passage appear to be more general than in fact it is. The οἱ λόγοι at *PH* 2.188 refers back to τοὺς κατὰ τῆς ἀποδείξεως λόγους at *PH* 2.187 and οἱ κατὰ τῆς ἀποδείξεως ἠρωτημένοι λόγοι at *PH* 2.185. The arguments Sextus compares to purgative drugs are the Sceptic's arguments against the existence of proof.

proves that there are no proofs thereby establishes by proof that there is at least one proof (*PH* 2.185). Sextus counters that a Sceptical argument against proof is an argument that (somehow) *both* proves its conclusion (that there are no proofs) *and* by doing so deprives itself of its status as a proof of that conclusion.[10] Sextus' comparison of Sceptical arguments against proof to purgative drugs, then, is motivated by what Sextus presents as a distinctive feature not of Sceptical arguments in general but only of *these* Sceptical arguments. Moreover, the distinctive feature of Sceptical arguments against proof in virtue of which Sextus compares them to purgative drugs is *not* any therapeutic effect these arguments might have on those exposed to them.

Finally, at *PH* 1.206 Sextus writes that all the Sceptical phrases uttered by the Sceptic can destroy themselves—'being cancelled along with what they are applied to, just as purgative drugs do not merely drain the humours from the body but drive themselves out too along with the humours'. A Sceptical phrase, or the utterance of a Sceptical phrase, shares a feature with Sceptical arguments against proof that we can call *self-application* (for it is not, strictly speaking, self-reference).[11] Call the Sceptical utterance 'Everything is inapprehensible' (E). In uttering (E) the Sceptic, according to Sextus, utters something that applies to itself. As a result, the Sceptic in uttering (E) does *not* utter it *as something apprehended or known*. Call the Sceptical utterance 'I determine nothing' (N). In uttering (N) the Sceptic utters something that applies to itself. Now (N) is equivalent to 'I assent to nothing' (*PH* 1.197). So the Sceptic in uttering (N) does *not* utter it *as something to which he assents*. Just as any argument the Sceptic offers against proof deprives itself of the status of a proof, so any utterance of a Sceptical phrase deprives itself of a certain status, e.g. as the utterance of something known or assented to by the Sceptic. The fact that some of the Sceptic's arguments and utterances have this feature of self-application is part of a conception of Scepticism not as therapeutic but rather as *non-dogmatic*. According to Sextus it is the dogmatic philosopher, not the Sceptic, who offers arguments as proofs and who makes utterances

[10] See also *M* 8.480–1. But note that Sextus also tries a different, and no more successful, defensive tactic at *M* 8.479. There he suggests that any argument the Sceptic offers against proof generates a conclusion that does not apply to itself. That is, the Sceptic's claim that there are no proofs is to be understood as the claim that there are no proofs besides the Sceptic's proofs that there are no proofs.

[11] And in fact at *PH* 2.188 Sextus himself indicates that self-application is a feature of both Sceptical arguments against proof and Sceptical phrases.

that express certain commitments, e.g. commitments to something as known or assented to. Now if this is the right way to understand Sextus' comparison of Sceptical arguments against proof and Sceptical phrases to purgative drugs, as I think it is, then that comparison has no significant implications for the Sceptic's attitude toward argument or reason in general.

The therapeutic strain in Scepticism is clearly in tension with those more central features of Scepticism that, I have argued, render Scepticism immune to the charge of anti-rationalism. The Sceptic who engages in philosophy as therapy—and, more specifically, the Sceptic who treats his arguments as therapeutic devices—cannot be engaged in the search for truth. The value of an argument appears to the Sceptic who is a therapist to be pragmatic rather than epistemic. A good argument is not an argument that establishes the truth of its conclusion and, by doing so, resolves a conflict between candidates for belief. A good argument is simply an argument that has the desired therapeutic effect—suspension of judgement—on the targeted beneficiary of the Sceptic's philanthropy. But someone who peddles Sceptical arguments as a panacea for the mental illness that dogmatism is thought to be has no concern for what, if any, relation those arguments bear to the truth. At most the Sceptic who is a therapist is concerned that his arguments *appear*, to others if not to himself, to establish the truth of their conclusions. And someone of this sort is engaged not in the search for truth but in a form of psychotherapy that exhibits a flagrant disregard for the truth.

Bibliography

ANCIENT WORKS

Cicero. *Academica* [*Acad.*], ed. J. S. Reid (London: Macmillan and Co., 1885).
—— *On Academic Scepticism*, trans. with introd. and notes Charles Brittain (Indianapolis: Hackett Publishing Co., 2006).
Diogenes Laertius [D.L.]. *Vitae Philosophorum*, ed. M. Marcovich, 2 vols. (Stuttgart and Leipzig: Teubner, 1999).
—— *Lives of Eminent Philosophers*, ed. and trans. R. D. Hicks, 2 vols. (Cambridge, Mass.: Harvard University Press, 1925).
Plutarch. *Against Colotes*, ed. and trans. Benedict Einarson and Phillip H. DeLacy, *Moralia*, vol. xiv (Cambridge, Mass: Harvard University Press, 1976).
Sextus Empiricus. *Opera*, ed. H. Mutschmann and J. Mau, 4 vols. (Leipzig: Teubner, 1954–6).
—— *Against the Logicians*, ed. and trans. Richard Bett (Cambridge: Cambridge University Press, 2005).
—— *Against the Ethicists*, trans. with introd. and commentary Richard Bett (Oxford: Clarendon Press, 1997).
—— *Outlines of Scepticism,* ed. and trans. Julia Annas and Jonathan Barnes (Cambridge: Cambridge University Press, 2000).
—— *The Skeptic Way: Sextus Empiricus'* Outlines of Pyrrhonism, trans. with introd. and commentary Benson Mates (New York: Oxford University Press, 1996).
—— *Sextus Empiricus: esquisses pyrrhoniennes*, introd., trans., and commentary Pierre Pellegrin (Paris: Éditions du Seuil, 1997).

COLLECTIONS OF ANCIENT TEXTS

Arnim, H. von, and Adler, M., eds. *Stoicorum Veterum Fragmenta*, 4 vols. (Leipzig: Teubner, 1903–5, 1924).
Long, A. A., and Sedley, D., eds. and trans. *The Hellenistic Philosophers*; vol. i: Translations of the principal sources, with philosophical commentary; vol. ii: Greek and Latin texts with notes and bibliography (Cambridge: Cambridge University Press, 1987).

MODERN WORKS

Allen, James. 'The Skepticism of Sextus Empiricus', *Aufstieg und Niedergang der römischen Welt* 36.4 (1990), 2582–607.

—— *Inference from Signs: Ancient Debates about the Nature of Evidence* (Oxford: Clarendon Press, 2001).

Annas, Julia. 'Doing without Objective Values: Ancient and Modern Strategies', in M. Schofield and G. Striker (eds.), *The Norms of Nature: Studies in Hellenistic Ethics* (Cambridge: Cambridge University Press, 1986), 3–29.

—— *The Morality of Happiness* (Oxford: Oxford University Press, 1993).

—— 'Scepticism Old and New', in M. Frede and G. Striker (eds.), *Rationality in Greek Thought* (Oxford: Clarendon Press, 1996), 239–54.

—— and Barnes, Jonathan. *The Modes of Scepticism: Ancient Texts and Modern Interpretations* (Cambridge: Cambridge University Press, 1985).

Bailey, Alan. *Sextus Empiricus and Pyrrhonean Scepticism* (Oxford: Oxford University Press, 2002).

Barnes, Jonathan. 'Ancient Skepticism and Causation', in Burnyeat (ed.), *The Skeptical Tradition*, 149–203.

—— 'The Beliefs of a Pyrrhonist', in Burnyeat and Frede (eds.), *The Original Sceptics*, 58–91.

—— 'Pyrrhonism, Belief, and Causation: Observations on the Scepticism of Sextus Empiricus', *Aufstieg und Niedergang der römischen Welt* 36.4 (1990), 2608–95.

—— *The Toils of Scepticism* (Cambridge: Cambridge University Press, 1990).

Barney, Rachel. 'Appearances and Impressions', *Phronesis* 37 (1992), 283–313.

Bett, Richard. *Pyrrho, his Antecedents, and his Legacy* (Oxford: Oxford University Press, 2000).

—— 'What Kind of Self Can a Greek Sceptic Have?', in P. Remes and J. Sihvola (eds.), *Ancient Philosophy of the Self* (Amsterdam: Springer, 2008), 139–54.

Bobzien, Susanne. *Determinism and Freedom in Stoic Philosophy* (Oxford: Clarendon Press, 1998).

Brennan, Tad. *Ethics and Epistemology in Sextus Empiricus* (New York: Garland Publishing, 1999).

Brunschwig, Jacques. *Papers in Hellenistic Philosophy*, trans. J. Lloyd (Cambridge: Cambridge University Press, 1994).

—— 'Sextus Empiricus and the *kritērion*: The Skeptic as Conceptual Legatee', in *Papers in Hellenistic Philosophy*, 224–43.

—— 'The ὅσον ἐπὶ τῷ λόγῳ Formula in Sextus Empiricus', in *Papers in Hellenistic Philosophy*, 244–58.

—— 'Cyrenaic Epistemology', in *The Cambridge History of Hellenistic Philosophy*, ed. K. Algra, J. Barnes, J. Mansfeld, and M. Schofield (Cambridge: Cambridge University Press, 1999), 251–9.

Burnyeat, Myles. 'Idealism and Greek Philosophy: What Descartes Saw and Berkeley Missed', *The Philosophical Review* 91 (1982), 3–40.

—— (ed.) *The Skeptical Tradition* (Berkeley and Los Angeles: University of California Press, 1983).

Burnyeat, Myles. 'Can the Sceptic Live his Scepticism?', in Burnyeat and Frede (eds.), *The Original Sceptics: A Controversy*, 25–57.

—— 'The Sceptic in his Time and Place,' in Burnyeat and Frede (eds.), *The Original Sceptics: A Controversy*, 92–126.

—— and Frede, Michael (eds.) *The Original Sceptics: A Controversy* (Indianapolis: Hackett Publishing Company, 1997).

Clifford, W. K. 'The Ethics of Belief', in his *Lectures and Essays*, ed. L. Stephen and F. Pollock, 2 vols. (London: Macmillan, 1879), ii. 177–211.

Cooper, John M. 'Arcesilaus: Socratic and Skeptic', in his *Knowledge, Nature, and the Good: Essays on Ancient Philosophy* (Princeton: Princeton University Press, 2004), 81–103.

Davidson, Donald. *Essays on Actions and Events* (Oxford: Clarendon Press, 1980).

—— 'Actions, Reasons, and Causes', in *Essays on Actions and Events*, 3–20.

—— 'How is Weakness of the Will Possible?', in *Essays on Actions and Events*, 21–42.

—— 'Intending', in *Essays on Actions and Events*, 83–102.

Everson, Stephen. 'The Objective Appearance of Pyrrhonism', in S. Everson (ed.), *Psychology* (Companions to Ancient Thought 2) (Cambridge: Cambridge University Press), 121–47.

Fine, Gail. 'Sceptical *Dogmata: Outlines of Pyrrhonism* I 13', *Methexis* 12 (2000), 81–105.

—— 'Subjectivity, Ancient and Modern: The Cyrenaics, Sextus, and Descartes', in Jon Miller and Brad Inwood (eds.), *Hellenistic and Early Modern Philosophy* (Cambridge: Cambridge University Press, 2003), 192–231.

—— 'Sextus and External World Scepticism', *Oxford Studies in Ancient Philosophy* 26 (2003), 341–85.

Fine, Kit. 'The Varieties of Necessity', in *Modality and Tense: Philosophical Papers* (New York: Oxford University Press, 2005), 235–60.

Frankfurt, Harry G. 'Freedom of the Will and the Concept of a Person', in his *The Importance of What We Care About* (Cambridge: Cambridge University Press, 1988), 11–25.

Frede, Michael. 'The Stoic Doctrine of the Affections of the Soul', in M. Schofield and G. Striker (eds.), *The Norms of Nature: Studies in Hellenistic Ethics* (Cambridge: Cambridge University Press, 1986), 93–110.

—— 'The Ancient Empiricists', in his *Essays in Ancient Philosophy* (Minneapolis: University of Minnesota Press, 1987), 243–60.

—— 'The Sceptic's Beliefs', in Burnyeat and Frede (eds.), *The Original Sceptics: A Controversy*, 1–24.

—— 'The Sceptic's Two Kinds of Assent and the Question of the Possibility of Knowledge', in Burnyeat and Frede (eds.), *The Original Sceptics: A Controversy*, 127–51.

—— 'The Stoic Conception of Reason', in K. J. Boudauris (ed.), *Hellenistic Philosophy*, vol. ii, (Athens, 1994), 50–63.

Grgic, Filip. 'Sextus Empiricus on the Goal of Skepticism', *Ancient Philosophy* 26 (2006), 141–60.

Hankinson, R. J. *The Sceptics* (London: Routledge, 1995).

Harman, Gilbert. 'Practical Reasoning', in *The Philosophy of Action*, ed. A. R. Mele (Oxford: Oxford University Press, 1997), 149–77.

Hume, David. *An Enquiry Concerning Human Understanding*, ed. Tom L. Beauchamp, Oxford Philosophical Texts (Oxford: Oxford University Press, 1999).

Inwood, Brad. *Ethics and Human Action in Early Stoicism* (Oxford: Clarendon Press, 1985).

Janáček, Karl. *Sextus Empiricus' Sceptical Methods* (Prague: Universita Karlova, 1972).

Johnsen, Bredo C. 'On the Coherence of Pyrrhonian Skepticism', *The Philosophical Review* 110 (2001), 521–62.

Kolodny, Niko. 'Why be Rational?' *Mind* 114 (2005), 509–63.

Loeb, Louis. 'Sextus, Descartes, Hume, and Peirce: On Securing Settled Doxastic States', *Noûs* 32 (1998), 205–30.

McPherran, Mark. 'Skeptical Homeopathy and Self-Refutation', *Phronesis* 32 (1987), 290–328.

—— '*Ataraxia* and *Eudaimonia* in Ancient Pyrrhonism', *Proceedings of the Boston Area Colloquium in Ancient Philosophy* 5 (1988), 135–71.

Morrison, Donald. 'The Ancient Sceptic's Way of Life', *Metaphilosophy* 21 (1990), 204–22.

Nussbaum, Martha C. *The Therapy of Desire: Theory and Practice in Hellenistic Ethics* (Princeton: Princeton University Press, 1994).

Obdrzalek, Suzanne. 'Living in Doubt: Carneades' *Pithanon* Reconsidered', *Oxford Studies in Ancient Philosophy* 31 (2006), 243–79.

Palmer, John. 'Skeptical Investigation', *Ancient Philosophy* 20 (2000), 351–73.

Sedley, David. 'The Motivation of Greek Skepticism', in Burnyeat (ed.), *The Skeptical Tradition*, 9–30.

Shields, Christopher J. 'Socrates among the Skeptics', in Paul A. Vander Waerdt (ed.), *The Socratic Movement* (Ithaca, NY: Cornell University Press, 1994), 341–66.

Smith, Michael. *The Moral Problem* (Oxford: Blackwell Publishing, 1994).

Sorabji, Richard. *Animal Minds & Human Morals: The Origins of the Western Debate* (Ithaca, NY: Cornell University Press, 1993).

Stough, Charlotte. 'Sextus Empiricus on Non-Assertion', *Phronesis* 29 (1984), 137–64.

Striker, Gisela. *Essays on Hellenistic Epistemology and Ethics* (Cambridge: Cambridge University Press, 1996).

—— 'Sceptical Strategies', in *Essays on Hellenistic Epistemology and Ethics*, 92–115.

Striker, Gisela. 'The Ten Tropes of Aenesidemus', in *Essays in Hellenistic Epistemology and Ethics*, 116–34.

——— '*Ataraxia*: Happiness as Tranquillity', in *Essays on Hellenistic Epistemology and Ethics*, 183–95.

——— 'Scepticism as a Kind of Philosophy', *Archiv für Geschichte der Philosophie* 83 (2001), 113–29.

——— 'Historical Reflections on Classical Pyrrhonism and Neo-Pyrrhonism', in Walter Sinnott-Armstrong (ed.), *Pyrrhonian Skepticism* (New York: Oxford University Press, 2004), 13–24.

Stroud, Barry. 'Scepticism, "Externalism," and Epistemology', in his *Understanding Human Knowledge: Philosophical Essays* (Oxford: Oxford University Press, 2000), 139–54.

Tsouna, Voula. *The Epistemology of the Cyrenaic School* (Cambridge: Cambridge University Press, 1983).

Velleman, J. David. 'Practical Reflection', *The Philosophical Review* 94 (1985), 33–61.

——— *The Possibility of Practical Reason* (Oxford: Clarendon Press, 2000).

——— 'On the Aim of Belief', in *The Possibility of Practical Reason*, 244–81.

Vogt, Katja. *Skepsis und Lebenspraxis: Das pyrrhonische Leben ohne Meinungen* (Freiburg and Munich: Aber Verlag, 1998).

——— 'Activity, Action, and Assent: On the Life of the Pyrrhonian Sceptic'. Unpublished manuscript.

Watson, Gary. 'Free Agency', in G. Watson (ed.), *Free Will*, 2nd edn. (Oxford: Oxford University Press, 2003), 337–51.

Williams, Bernard. *Descartes: The Project of Pure Inquiry* (London: Penguin Books, 1978).

——— *Shame and Necessity* (Berkeley and Los Angeles: University of California Press, 1993).

Williams, Michael. 'Scepticism without Theory', *Review of Metaphysics* 41 (1988), 547–88.

Woodruff, Paul. 'Aporetic Pyrrhonism', *Oxford Studies in Ancient Philosophy* 6 (1988), 139–68.

Index of Passages

General Index

9 780199 557905